EASY PIANO

THE BEST LOVE SONGS EVER

ISBN 0-7935-6016-0

HAL•LEONARD®
CORPORATION

7777 W. BLUEMOUND RD. P.O. BOX 13819 MILWAUKEE, WI 53213

CONTENTS

THE BEST LOVE SONGS EVER

ALWAYS

Words and Music by
IRVING BERLIN

I'll be lov - ing you   al - ways

with   a love that's true

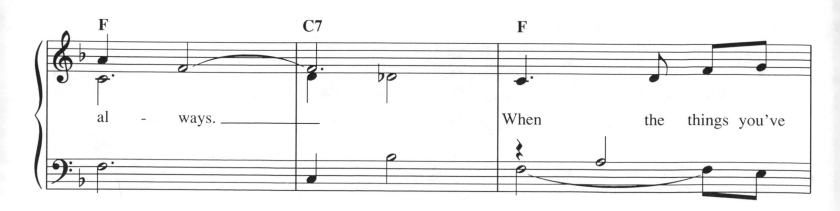

al - ways.   When   the things you've

5

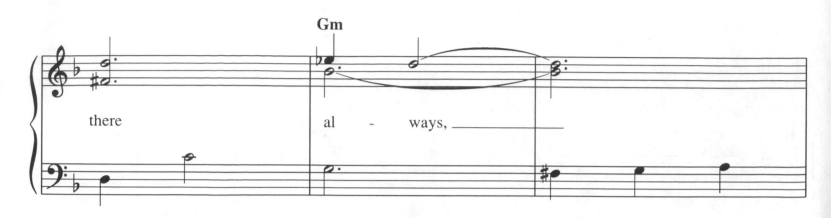

there   al - ways, _____

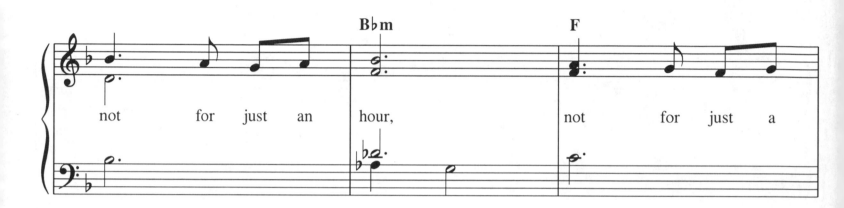

not   for   just   an   hour,   not   for   just   a

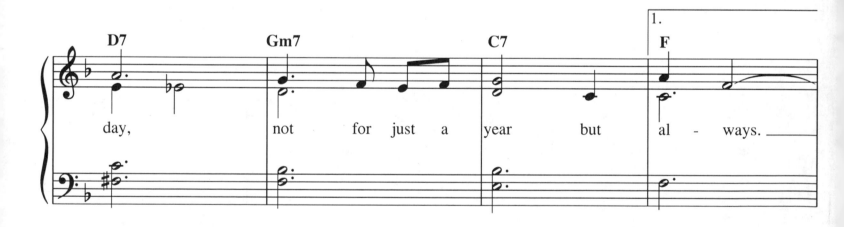

day,   not   for   just   a   year   but   al - ways. _____

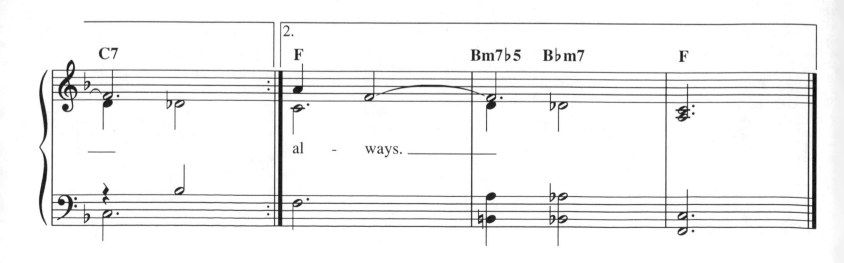

_____   al - ways. _____

AND I LOVE HER

Words and Music by JOHN LENNON
and PAUL McCARTNEY

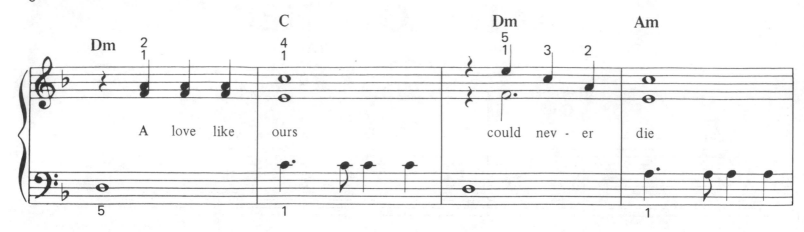

A love like ours could nev - er die

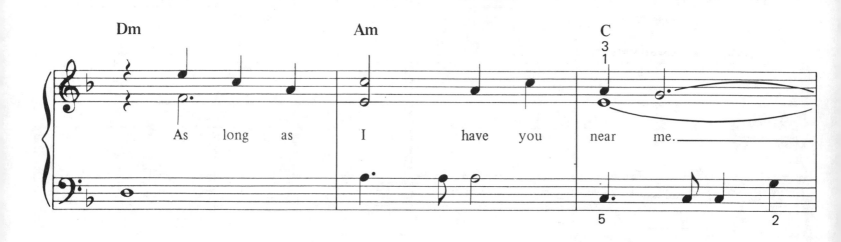

As long as I have you near me.

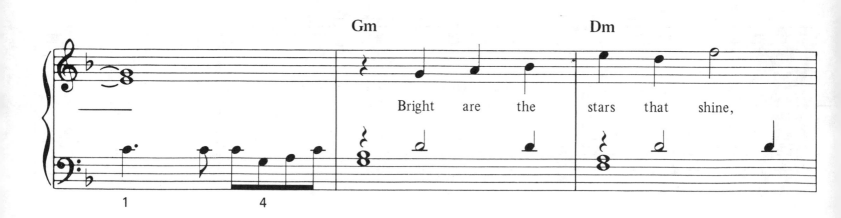

Bright are the stars that shine,

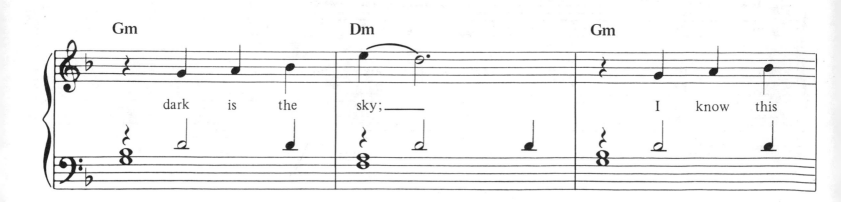

dark is the sky; I know this

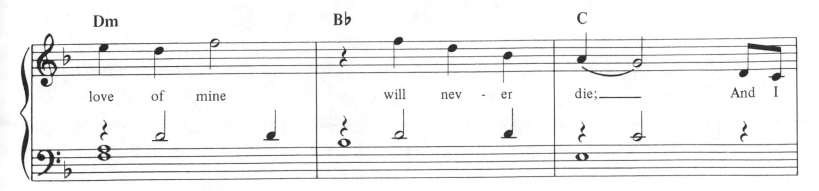

love of mine will nev - er die;_____ And I

love her._____

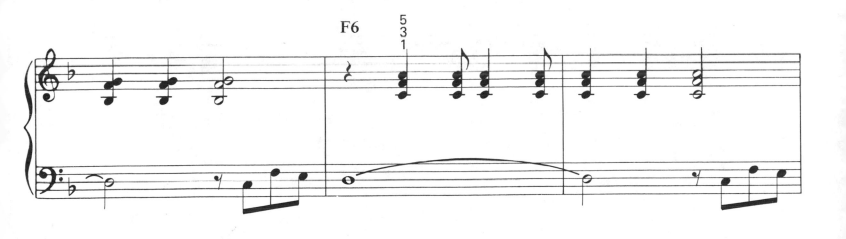

slowing

AND I LOVE YOU SO

Words and Music by
DON McLEAN

how   lone -ly   life   has   been,
and   once   a   page   is   read,

but   life   be - gan   a -
all   but   love   is

gain,
dead.

the   day   you   took   my
That   is   my   be -

hand.
lief.   }

And,   yes   I   know   how

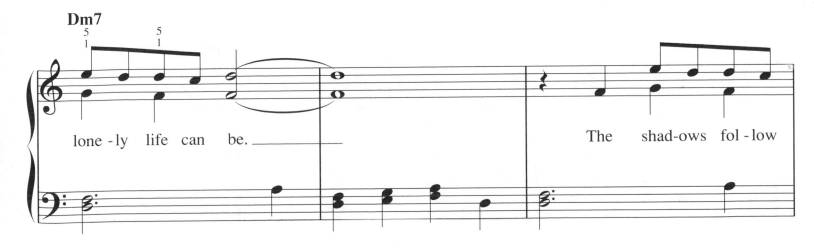

lone -ly   life   can   be. _____

The   shad -ows   fol -low

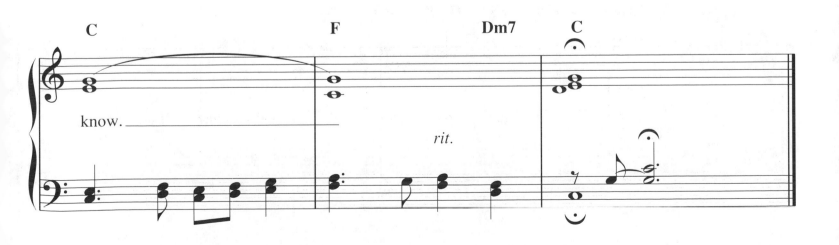

ANNIVERSARY SONG

By AL JOLSON
and SAUL CHAPLIN

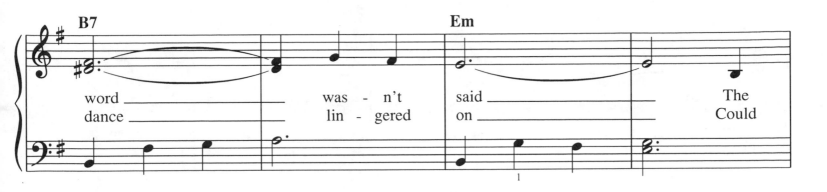

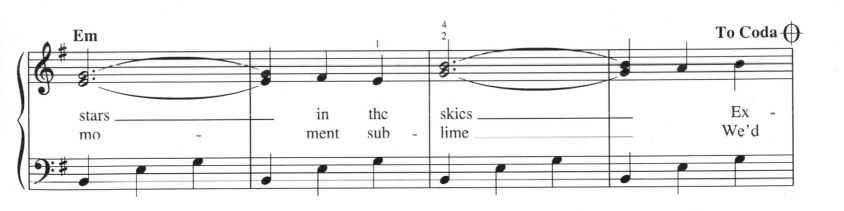

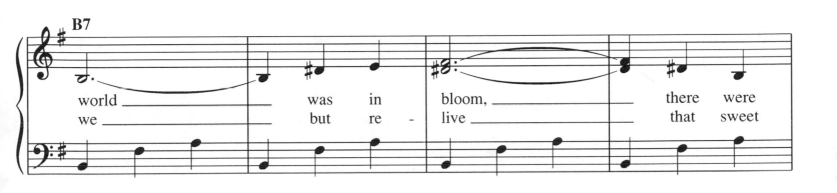

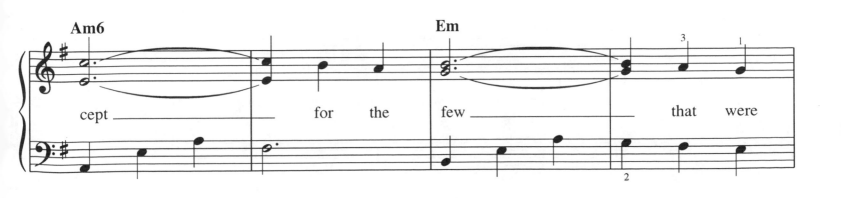

16

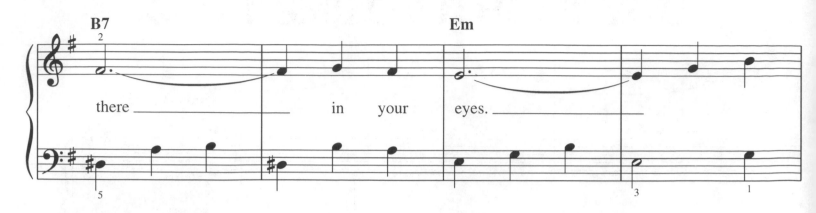

there _____ in your eyes. _____

Dear, as I held you so close in my arms,

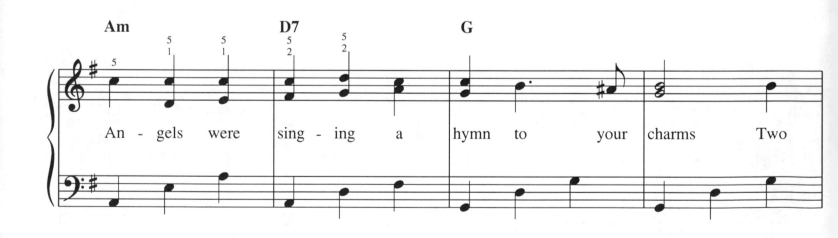

An - gels were sing - ing a hymn to your charms Two

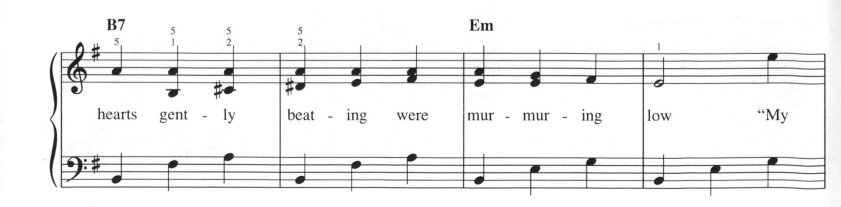

hearts gent - ly beat - ing were mur - mur - ing low "My

dar - ling,   I   love   you   so."____

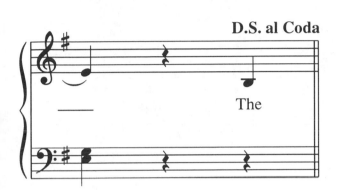

____   The

find _____

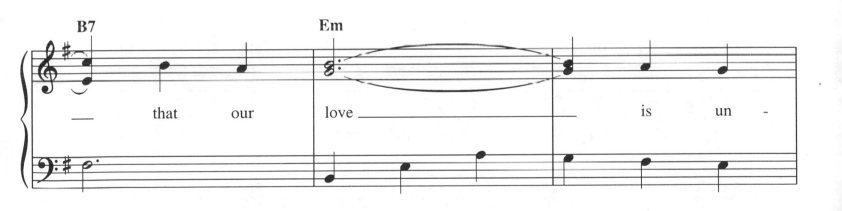

____   that   our   love _____   is   un -

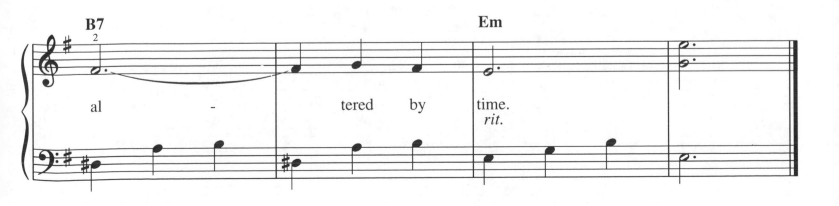

al   -   tered   by   time.
rit.

ANYTIME YOU NEED A FRIEND

Words and Music by MARIAH CAREY
and WALTER AFANASIEFF

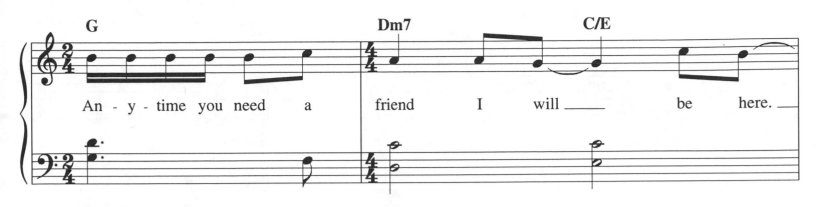

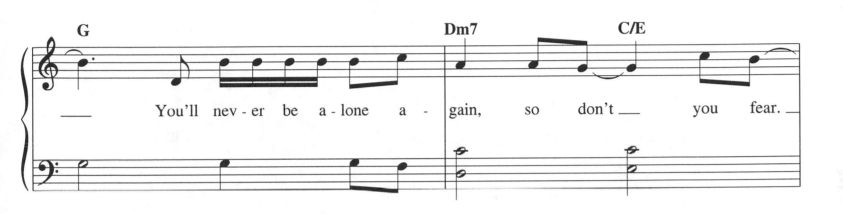

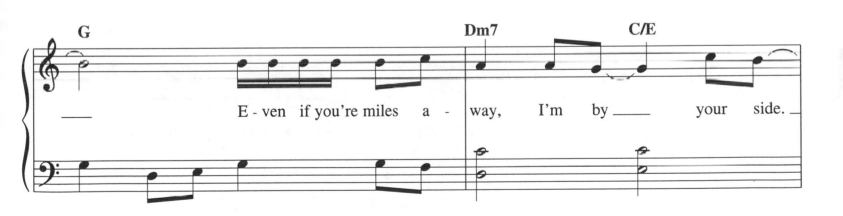

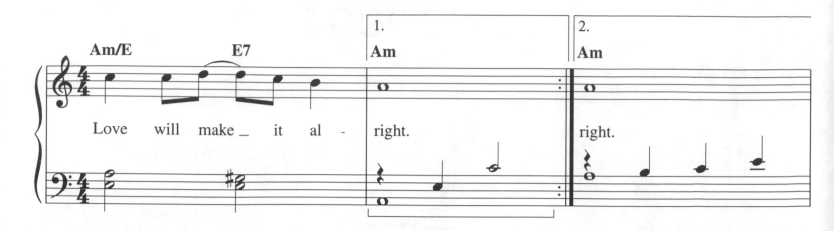

Love will make __ it al - right. right. right.

If you just be - lieve __ in me I will love you end -

- less - ly. Take my hand. Take me in - to your heart. __

I'll be there for - ev - er, ba - by. I won't let go. __ I'll nev - er let go. _____ An - y - time you need a

BEAUTIFUL IN MY EYES

Words and Music by
JOSHUA KADISON

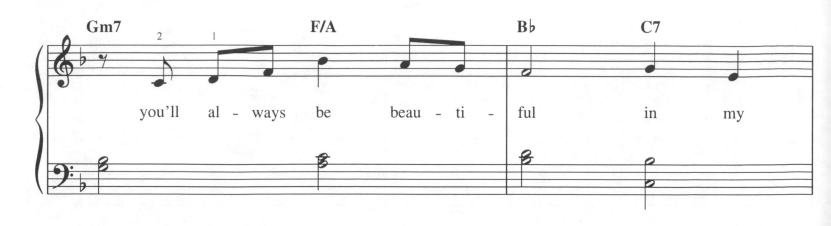

you'll al - ways be beau - ti - ful in my

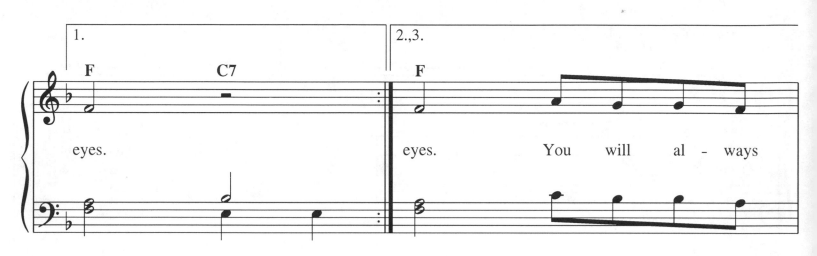

1.
eyes.

2.,3.
eyes. You will al - ways

be beau - ti - ful in my eyes. _____

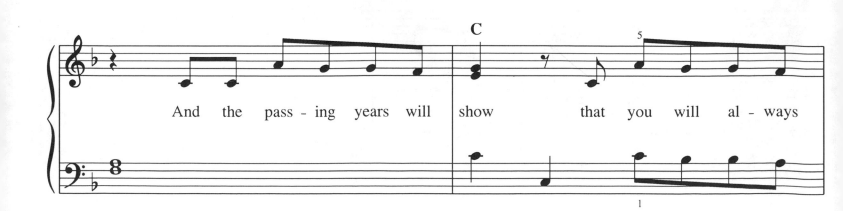

And the pass - ing years will show that you will al - ways

grow _ ev - er more beau - ti - ful ____ in my eyes.

When there are

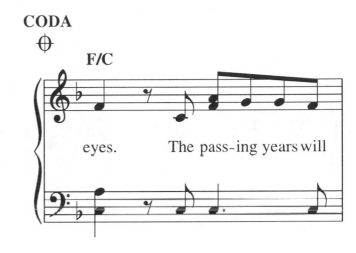

eyes.   The pass-ing years will

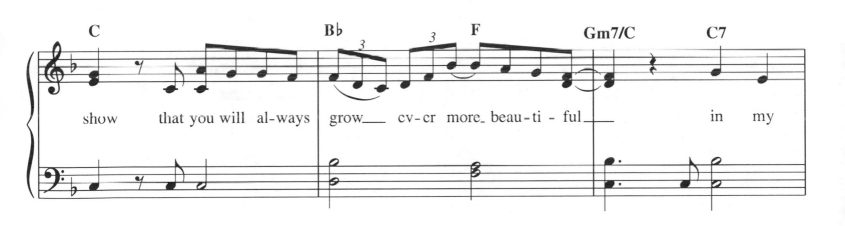

show   that you will al-ways grow ___ ev-er more _ beau-ti - ful ____   in my

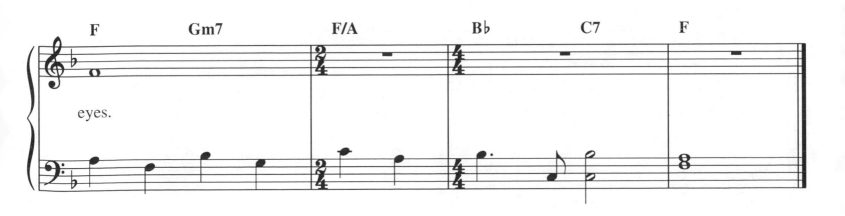

eyes.

CAN YOU FEEL THE LOVE TONIGHT

from Walt Disney Pictures' THE LION KING

Music by ELTON JOHN
Lyrics by TIM RICE

There's a calm_ sur - ren - der
There's a time_ for ev - 'ry - one,

to the rush_ of day,
if they on - ly learn

when the heat_ of the roll - ing world
that the twist - ing ka - lei - do - scope

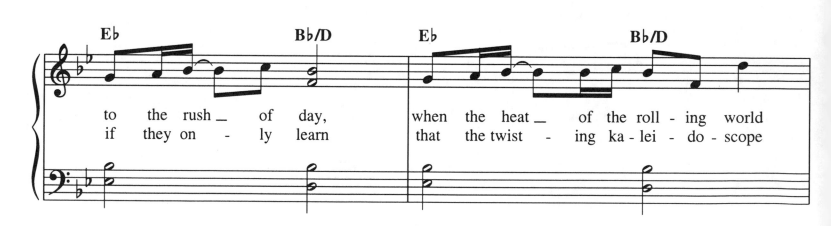

can be turned_ a - way.
moves us all ____ in turn.

An en - chant - ed mo - ment,
There's a rhyme_ and rea - son

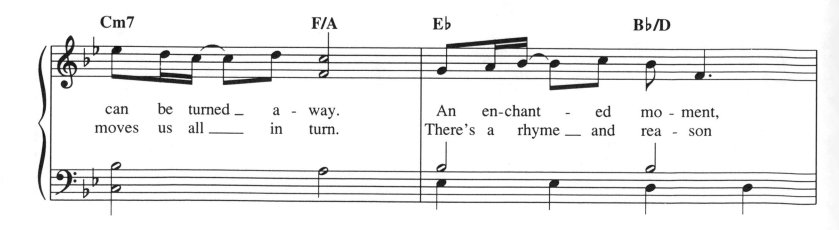

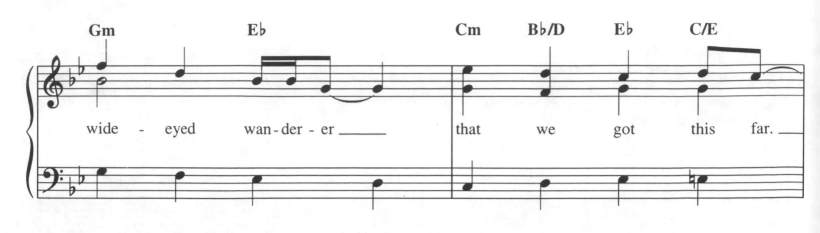

wide - eyed wan - der - er _____ that we got this far.

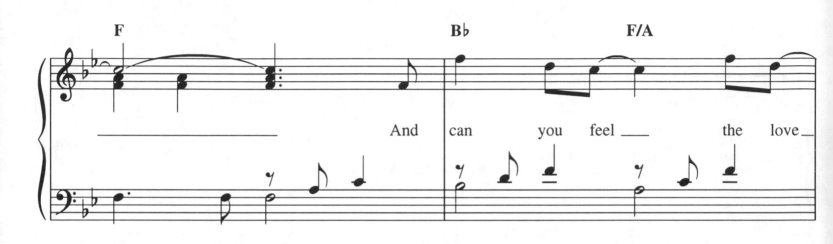

_____ And can you feel _____ the love _____

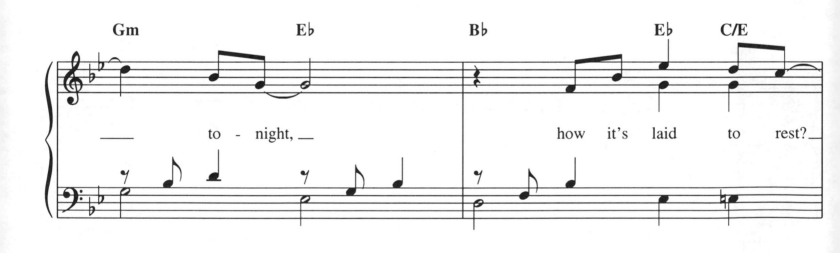

_____ to - night, _____ how it's laid to rest?

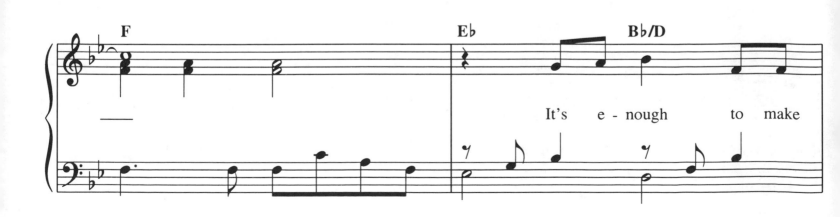

_____ It's e - nough to make

CAN'T HELP FALLING IN LOVE

Words and Music by GEORGE DAVID WEISS,
HUGO PERETTI and LUIGI CREATORE

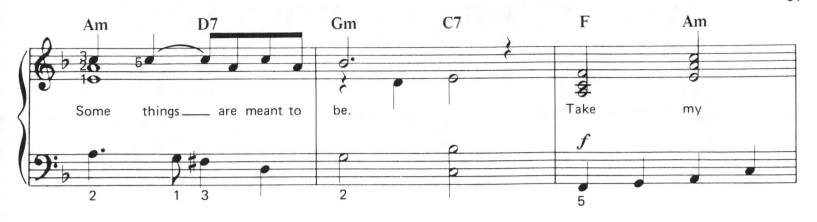

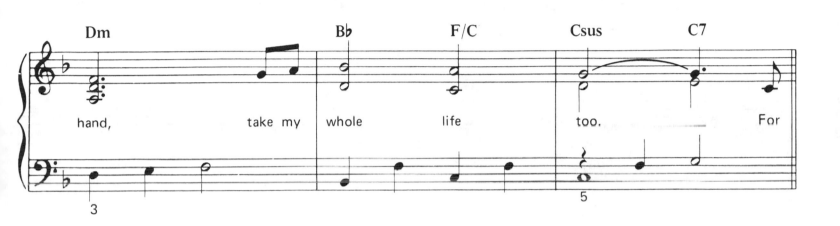

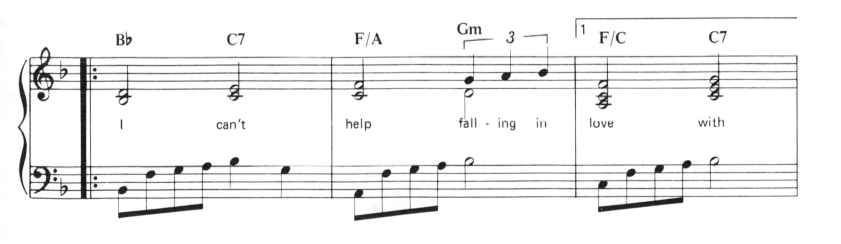

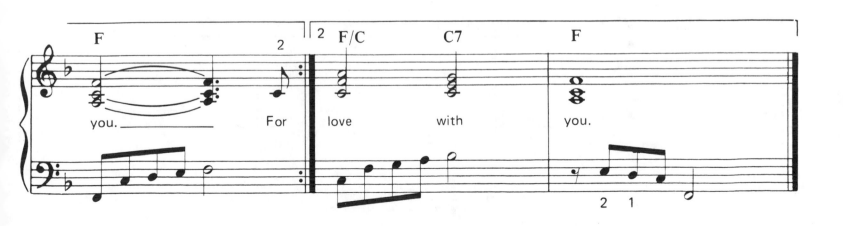

CAN'T SMILE WITHOUT YOU

Words and Music by CHRIS ARNOLD,
DAVID MARTIN and GEOFF MORROW

33

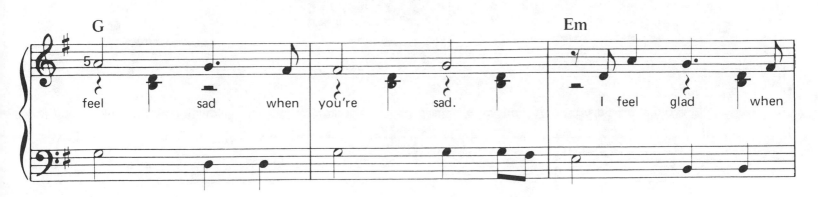

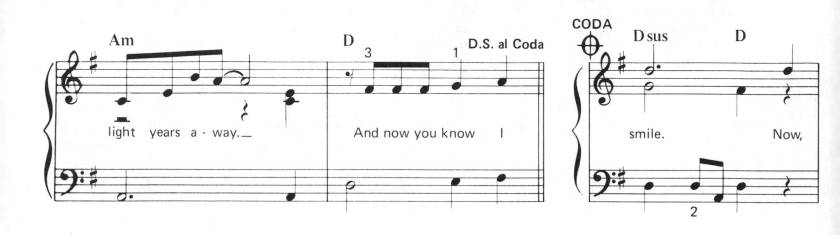

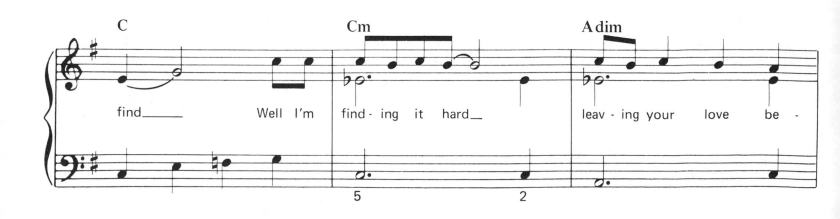

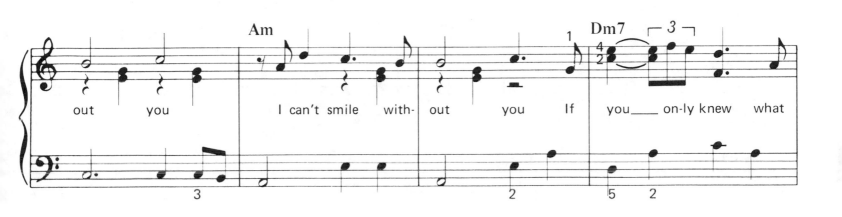

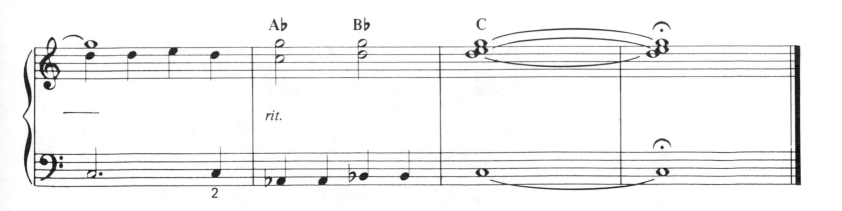

(They Long to Be)
CLOSE TO YOU

Lyric by HAL DAVID
Music by BURT BACHARACH

Slowly with a steady beat

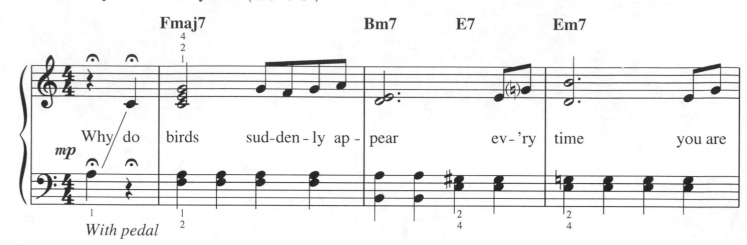

Why do birds sud-den-ly ap - pear ev-'ry time you are

With pedal

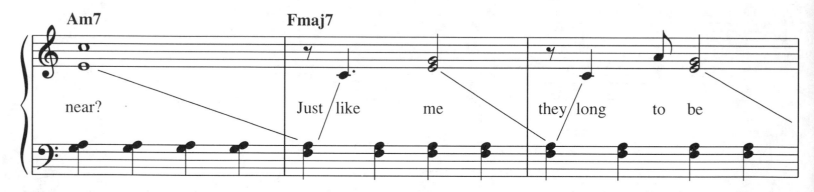

near? Just like me they long to be

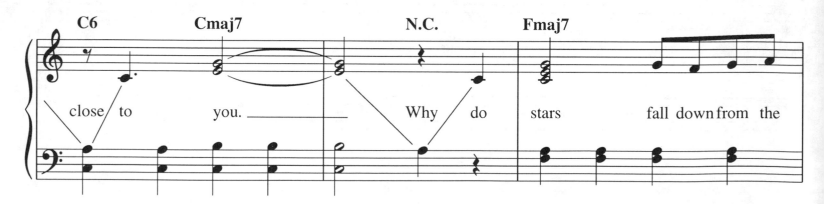

close to you. Why do stars fall down from the

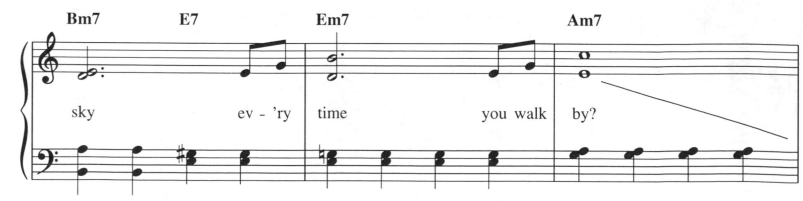

sky ev-'ry time you walk by?

37

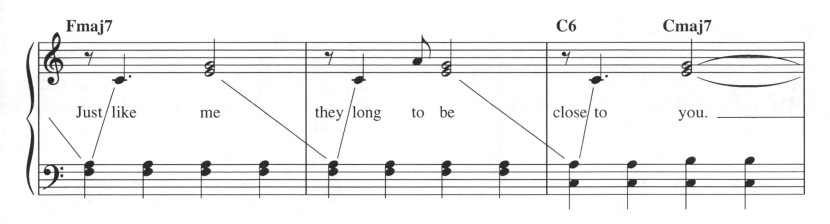

Just like me they long to be close to you. ___

___ On the day that you were born the an-gels got to-geth-er and de-

cid-ed to cre-ate a dream come true. So, they sprink-led moon dust in your hair of

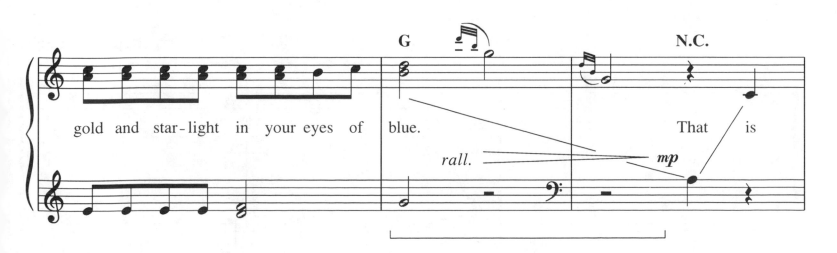

gold and star-light in your eyes of blue. That is

38

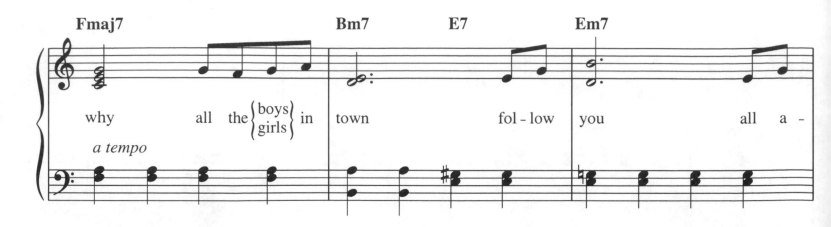

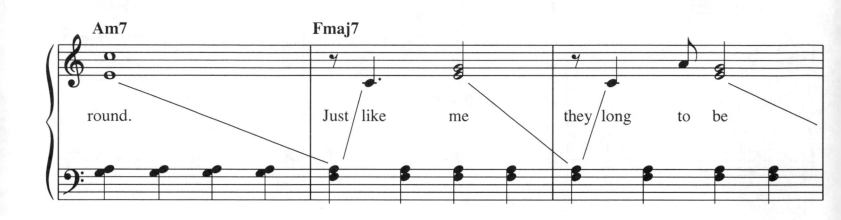

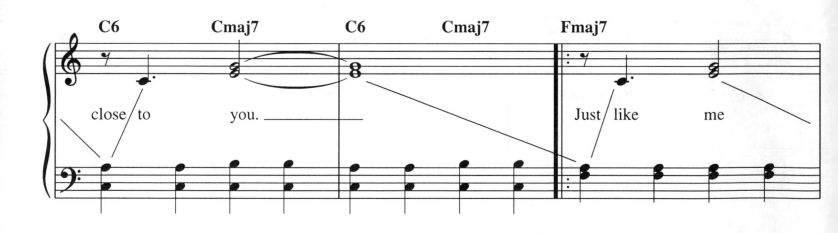

Repeat and Fade

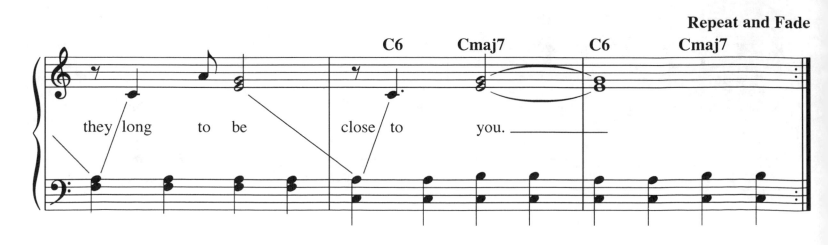

COULD I HAVE THIS DANCE

Words and Music by WAYLAND HOLYFIELD
and BOB HOUSE

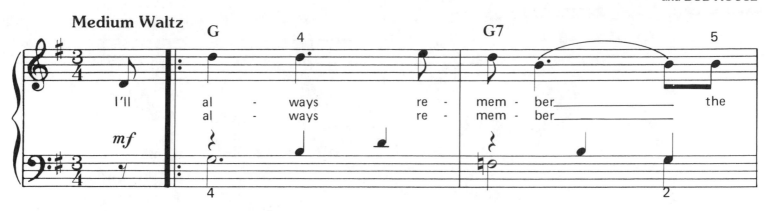

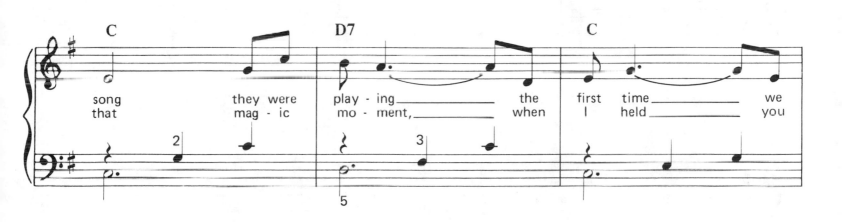

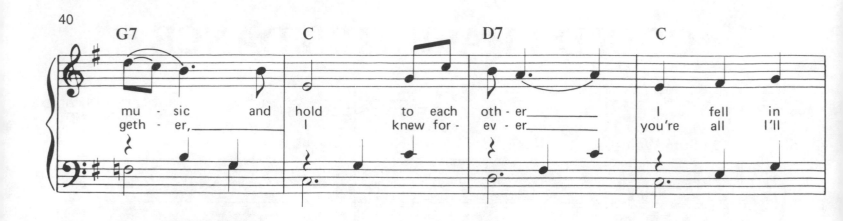

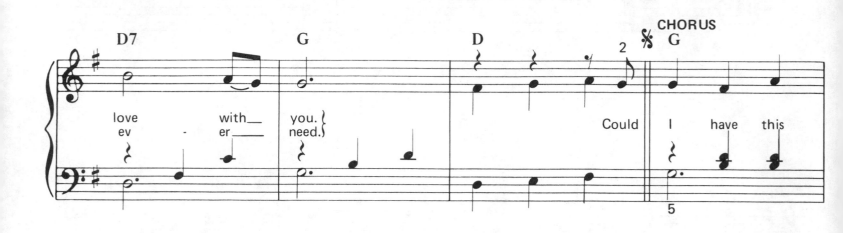

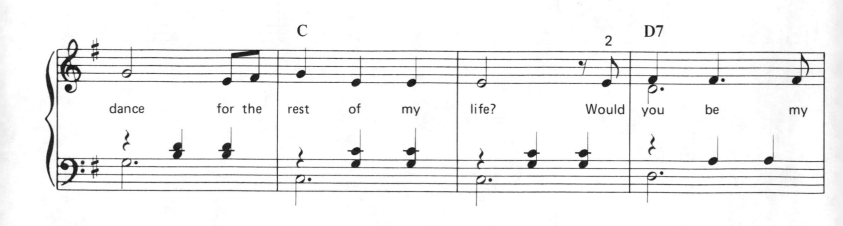

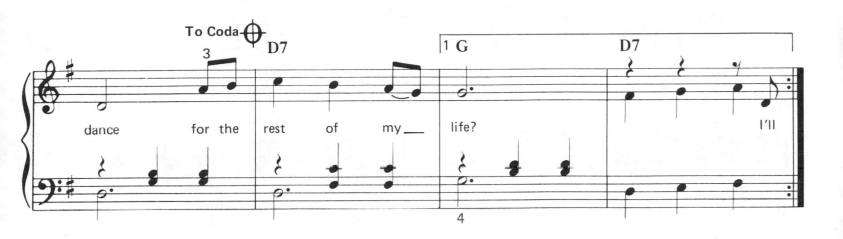
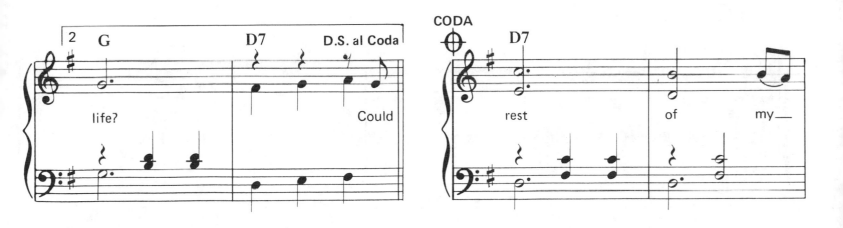
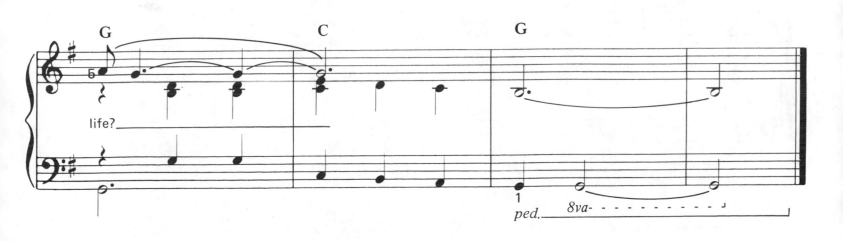

DON'T KNOW MUCH

Words and Music by BARRY MANN,
CYNTHIA WEIL and TOM SNOW

I don't know much, but I know I love you, _____ and that may be _____ all I need to

ENDLESS LOVE

Words and Music by
LIONEL RICHIE

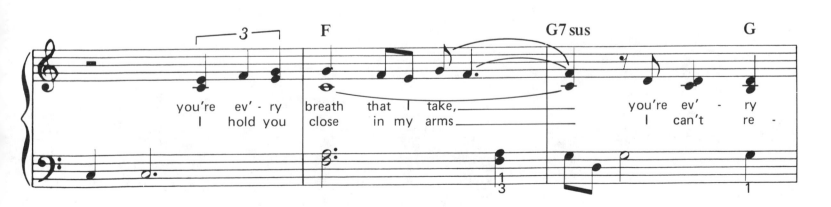

step I make.___
sist your charms.___
cresc.
And
And I,
love, *mf*

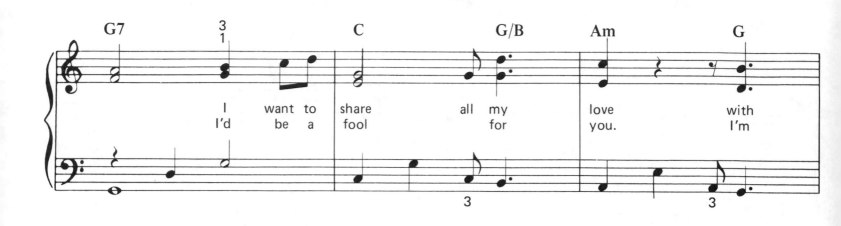

I want to
I'd be a
share all my
fool for
love you.
with I'm

you,___
sure___
no one else
you___ know
will___ do.___
I don't mind,___

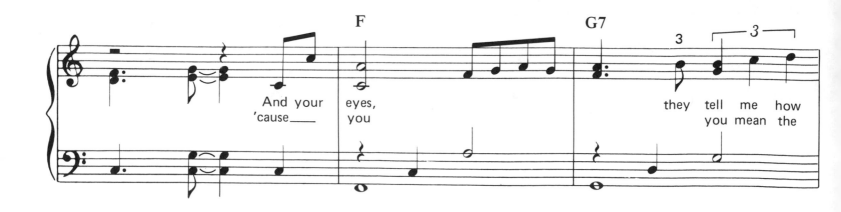

And your eyes,
'cause___ you
they tell me how
you mean the

FALLING IN LOVE WITH LOVE

from THE BOYS FROM SYRACUSE

Words by LORENZ HART
Music by RICHARD RODGERS

Moderate Waltz Tempo

53

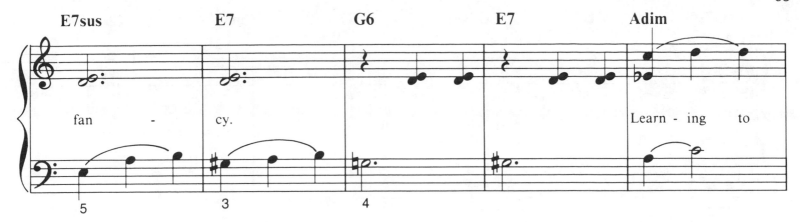

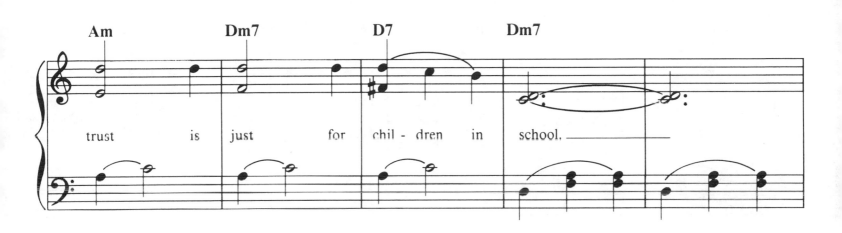

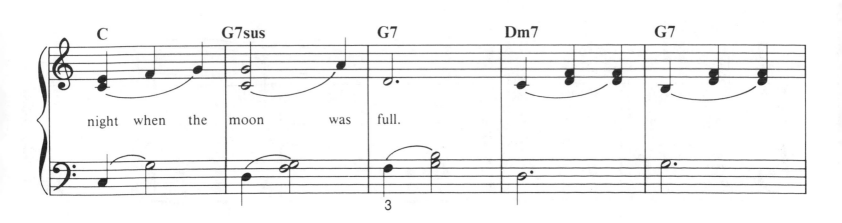

54

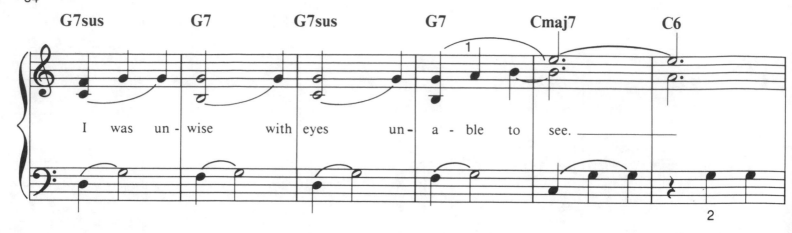

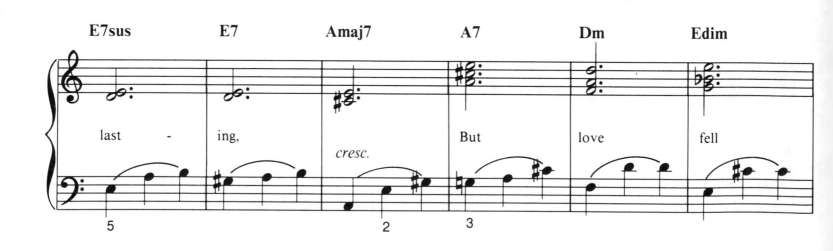

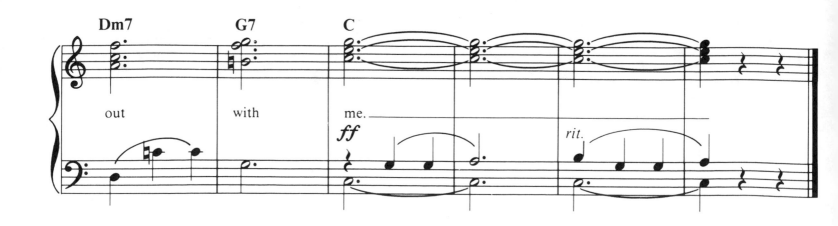

THE FIRST TIME
EVER I SAW YOUR FACE

Words and Music by
EWAN MacCOLL

With pedal

The first time _____ _____ ev - er I
The first time _____ _____ ev - er I
The first time _____ _____ ev - er I

saw   your face, _____ _____ I thought _____ the sun _____
kissed   your mouth, _____ _____ I felt _____ the earth _____
lay   with you _____ _____ and felt _____ your heart _____

rose _____ in your eyes, _____
move _____ in my hand, _____
so _____ close to mine, _____

and the moon ____ and the stars ____ were the
like the trem - bling heart ____ of a
and I knew ____ our joy ____ would

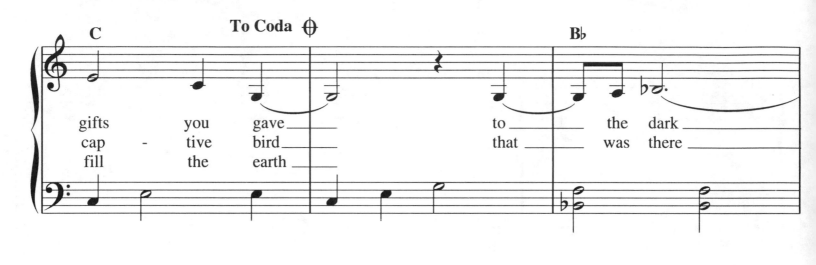

gifts you gave ____ to ____ the dark ____
cap - tive bird ____ that ____ was there ____
fill the earth ____

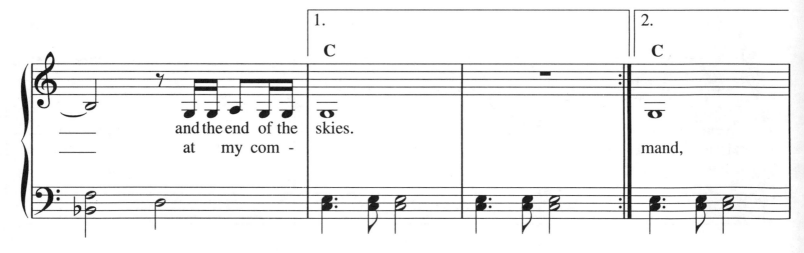

1.
____ and the end of the skies.
at my com -

2.
mand,

D.S. al Coda

my love.

CODA

and last

till the end of time, my love.

The first time ever I saw your

your face, your face,

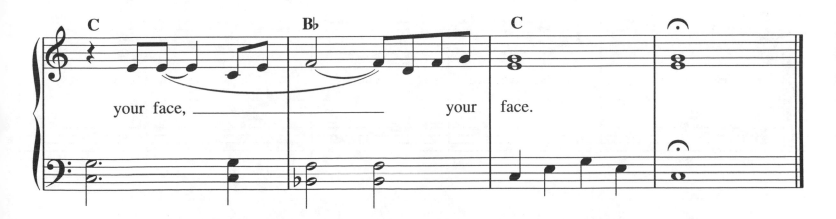

your face, your face.

FEELINGS
(¿Dime?)

English Words and Music by MORRIS ALBERT
Spanish lyric by THOMAS FUNDORA

Slowly, with expression

Both hands 8va (1st time only) - - - - - - - - - -

Feel - ings, nothing more than feel - ings,
Tear - drops, roll - ing down on my face,

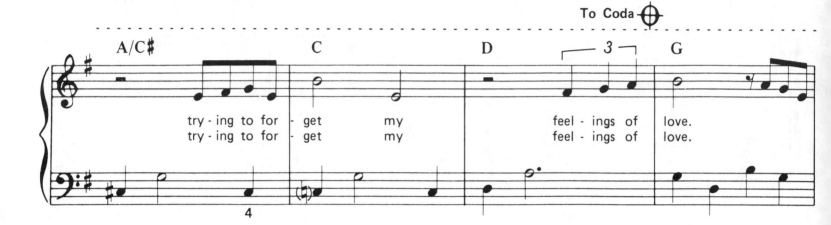

try - ing to for - get my feel - ings of love.
try - ing to for - get my feel - ings of love.

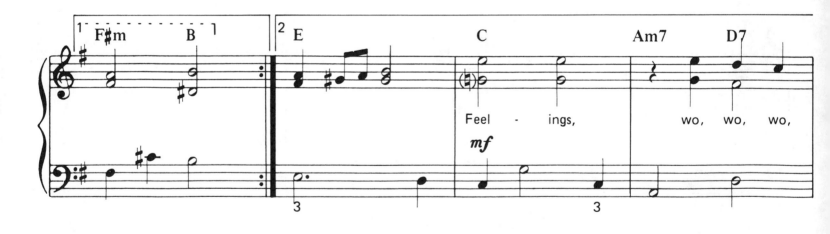

Feel - ings, wo, wo, wo,

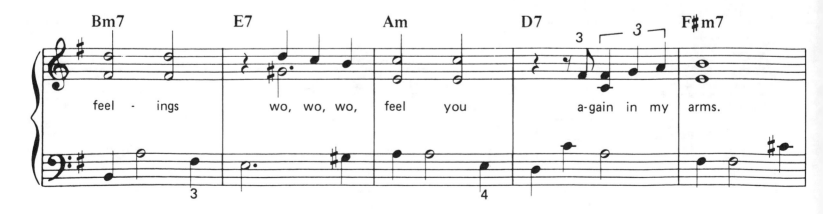

feel - ings wo, wo, wo, feel you a - gain in my arms.

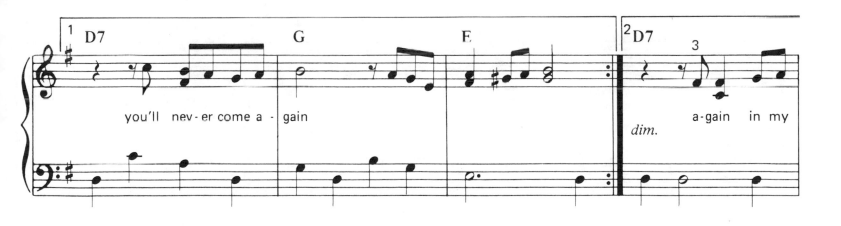

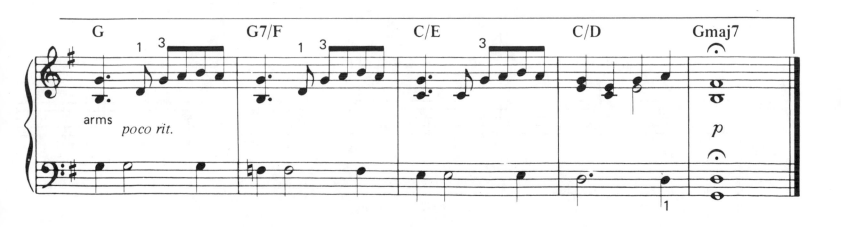

FOR ALL WE KNOW
from the Motion Picture LOVERS AND OTHER STRANGERS

Words by ROBB WILSON and JAMES GRIFFIN
Music by FRED KARLIN

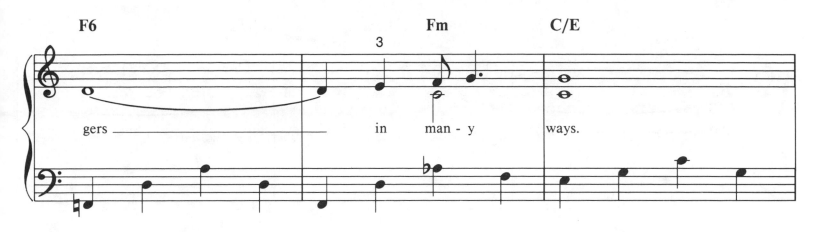

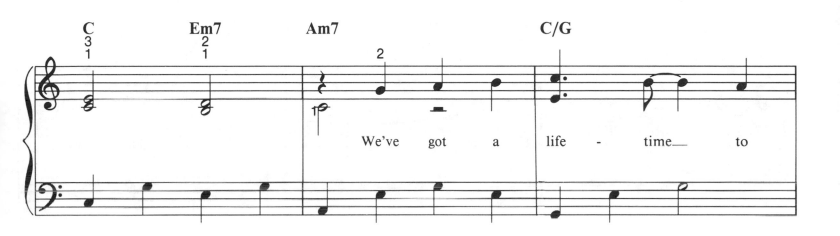

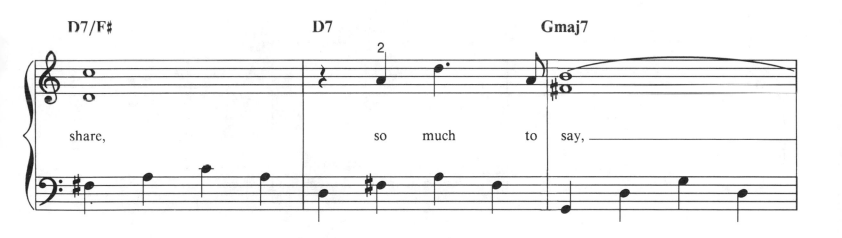

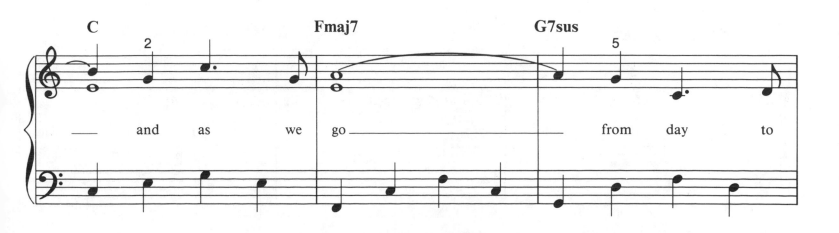

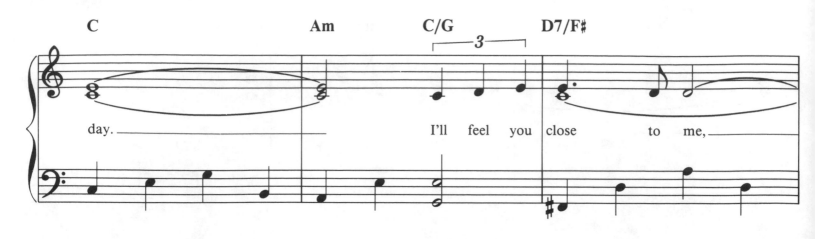

day. _____ I'll feel you close to me, _____

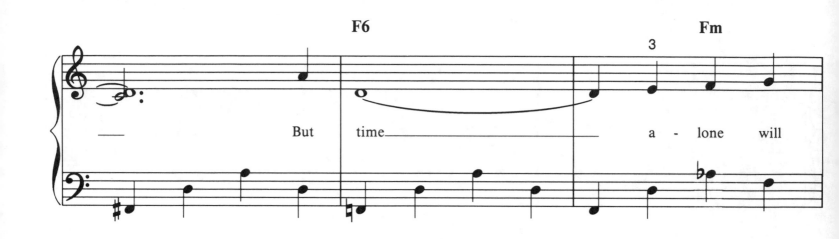

_____ But time _____ a - lone will

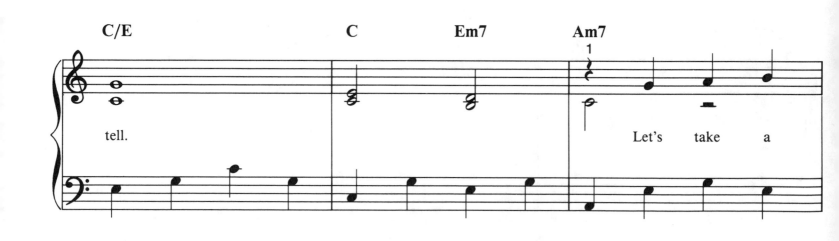

tell. Let's take a

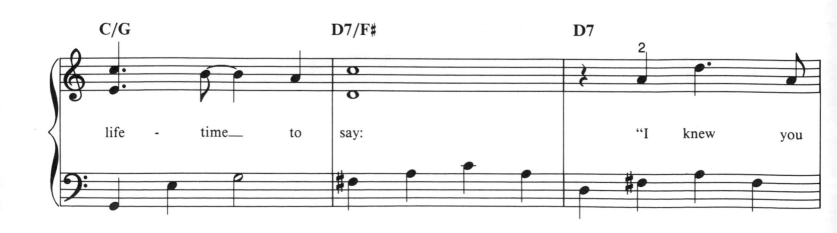

life - time to say: "I knew you

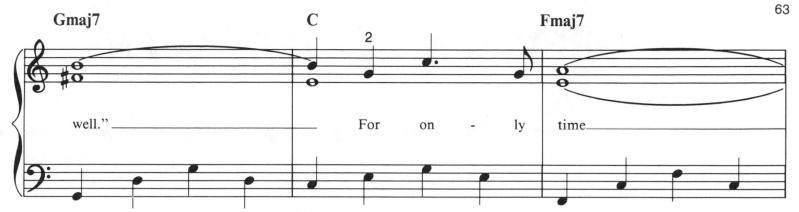

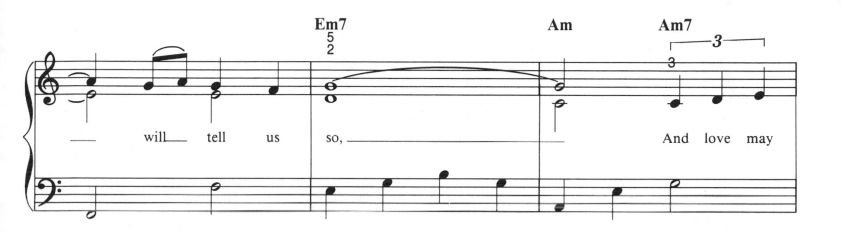

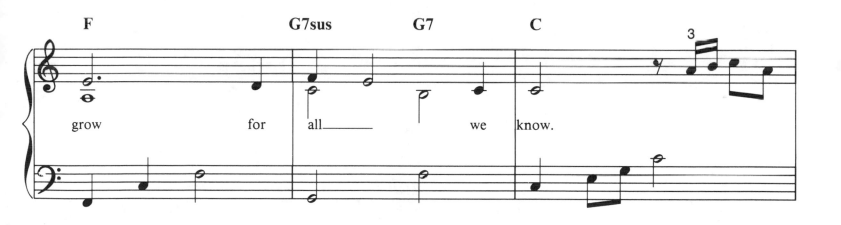

FOREVER AND EVER, AMEN

Words and Music by DON SCHLITZ
and PAUL OVERSTREET

Moderate Country

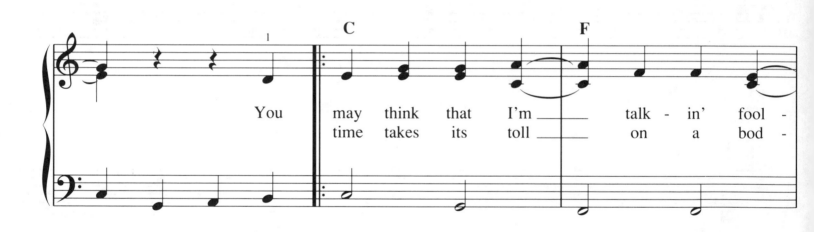

You may think that I'm _____ talk - in' fool -
time takes its toll _____ on a bod -

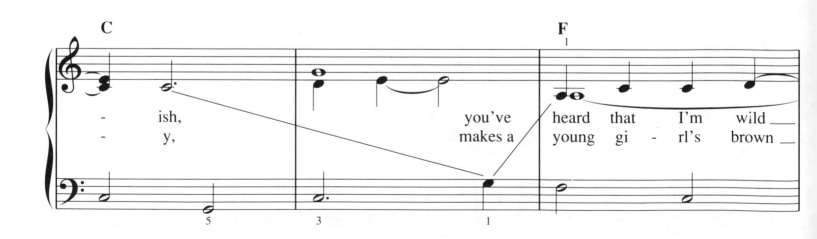

- ish, you've heard that I'm wild _____
- y, makes a young gi - rl's brown _____

65

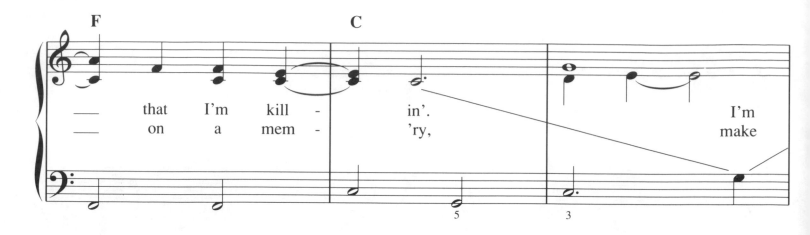

un - til the day that I ___ die ___ Oh, ba - by
-ten ev - 'ry wom - an, but you. ___ Oh, dar - lin'

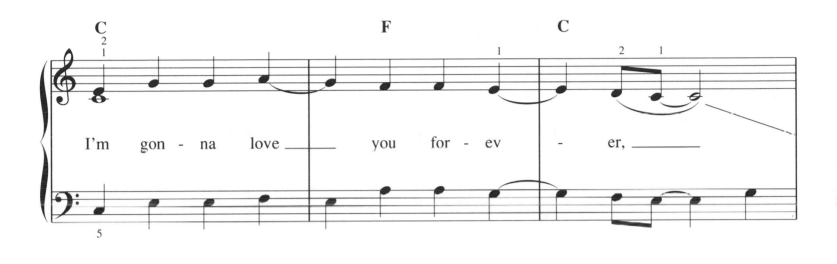

I'm gon - na love ___ you for - ev ___ - er, ___

for - ev - er and ev - ___ er, a - men.

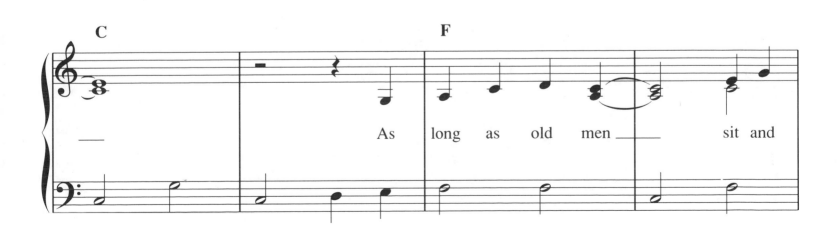

As long as old men ___ sit and

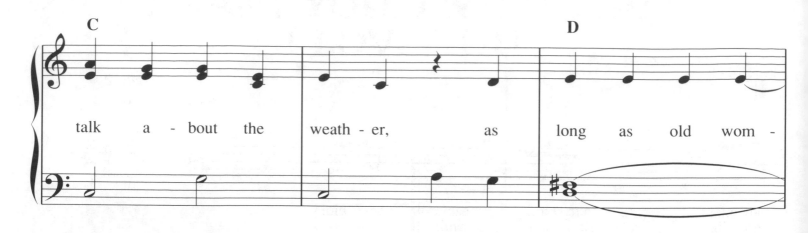

talk a - bout the weath - er, as long as old wom -

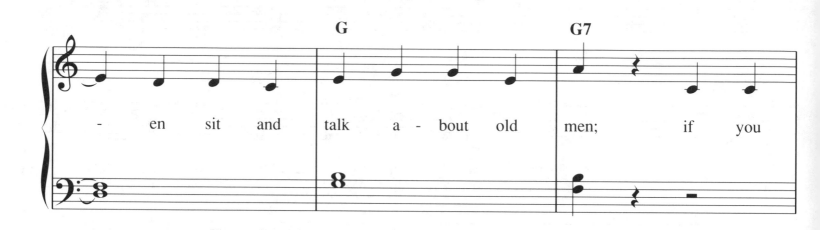

- en sit and talk a - bout old men; if you

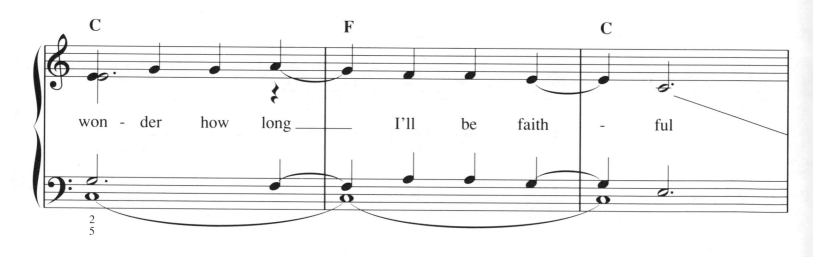

won - der how long _____ I'll be faith - ful

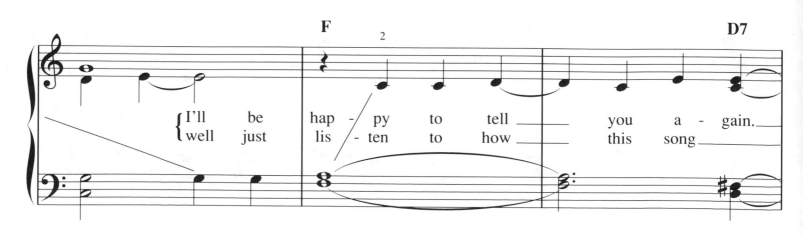

I'll be hap - py to tell _____ you a - gain.
well just lis - ten to how _____ this song _____

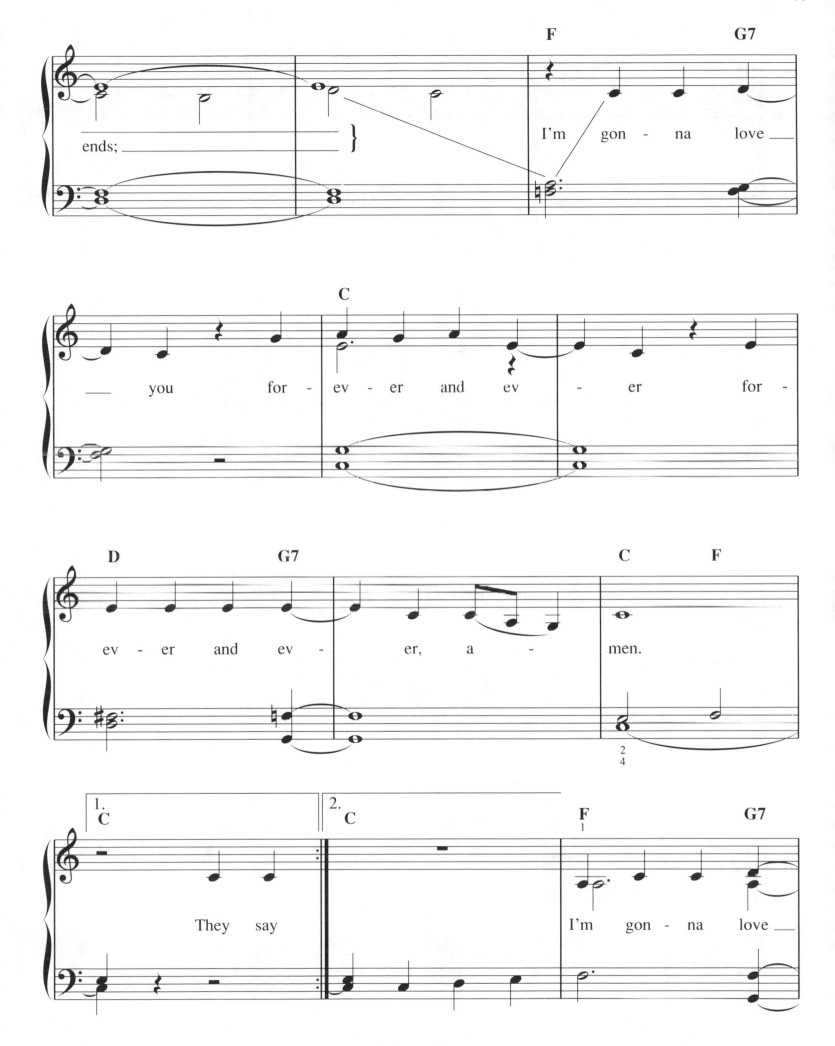

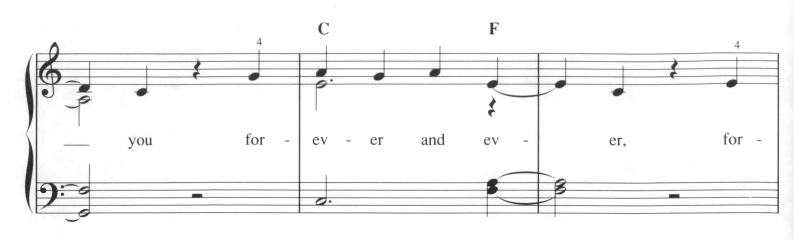

you for - ev - er and ev - er, for -

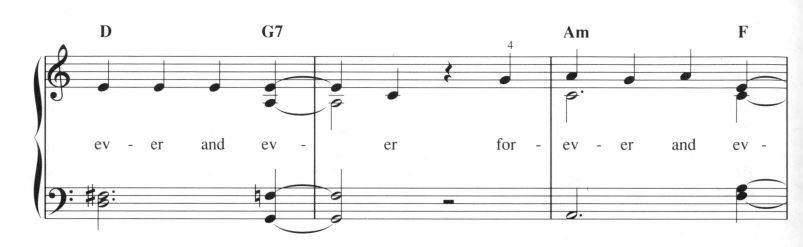

ev - er and ev - er for - ev - er and ev -

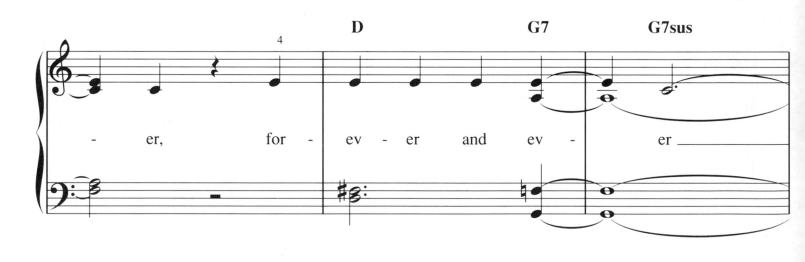

- er, for - ev - er and ev - er

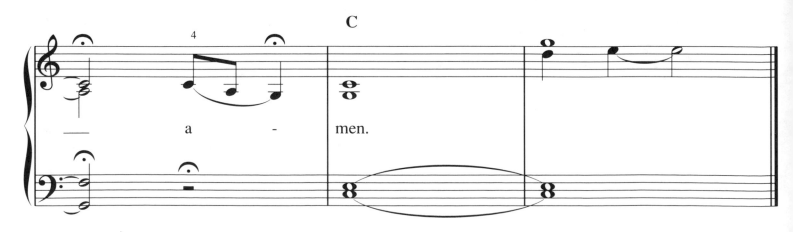

a - men.

HOW DEEP IS YOUR LOVE

Words and Music by BARRY GIBB,
MAURICE GIBB and ROBIN GIBB

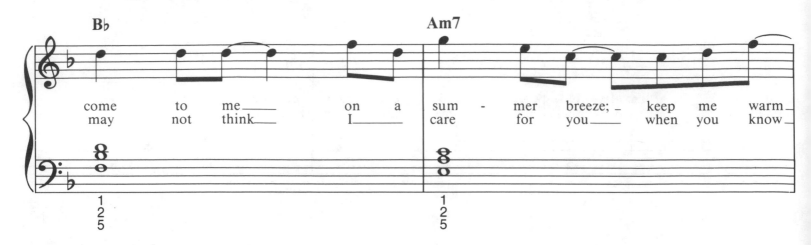

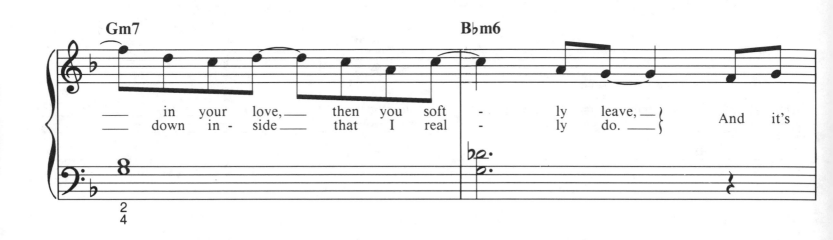

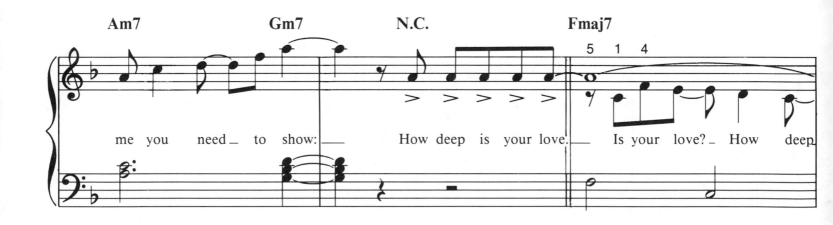

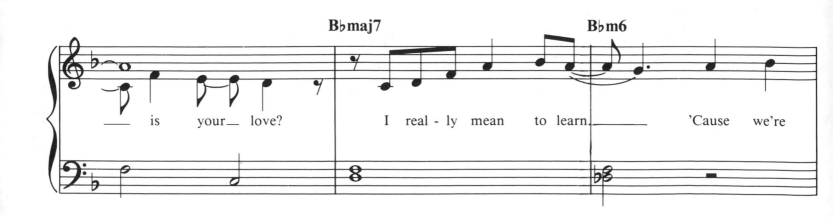

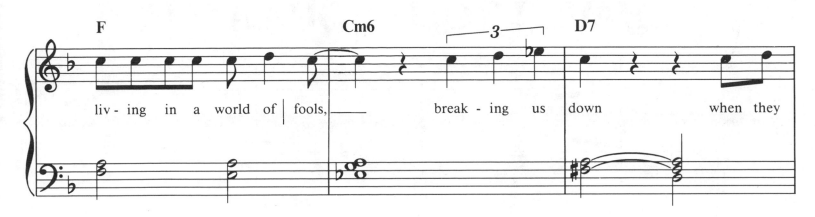

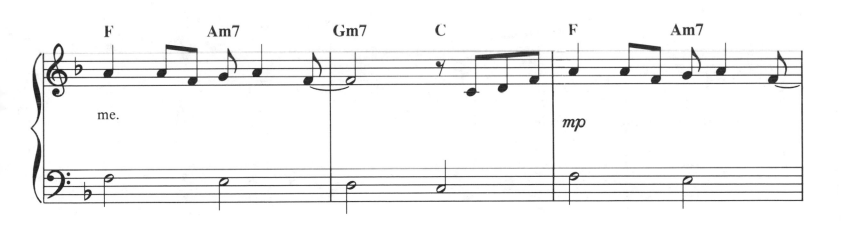

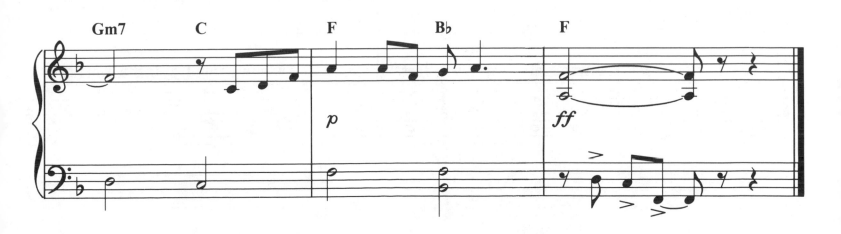

HAVE I TOLD YOU LATELY

Words and Music by
VAN MORRISON

Have I told you late-ly that I love you?_____ Have I told you there's no one else a - bove you?_____ Fill my heart with glad-ness, take a-way all my sad - ness, ease my trou-bles that's what you

like the sun.

And at the end of the day

we should give thanks and pray

to the one, ___

to the one. _ Have I

to the one. _ And have I

told you late-ly that I

love you? Have I

told you there's no one else a - bove you? ___

I JUST FALL IN LOVE AGAIN

Words and Music by LARRY HERBSTRITT, STEPHEN, H. DORFF,
GLORIA SKLEROV and HARRY LLOYD

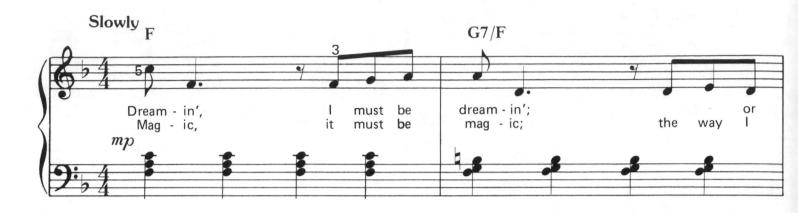

Dream - in', I must be dream - in'; or the way I
Mag - ic, it must be mag - ic;

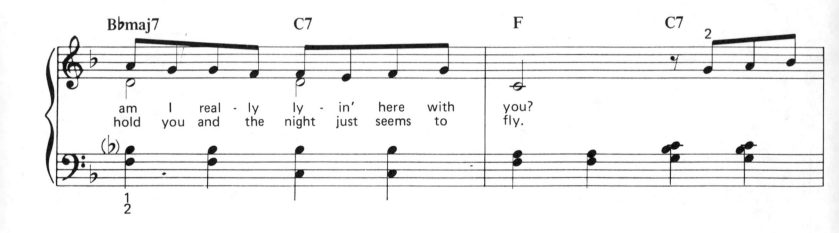

am I real - ly ly - in' here with you?
hold you and the night just seems to fly.

Ba - by, you take me in your arms and
Eas - y for you to take me to a star,

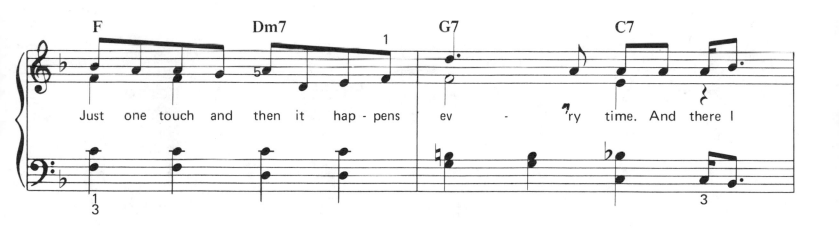

do, I can't help my-self I fall in love with you.

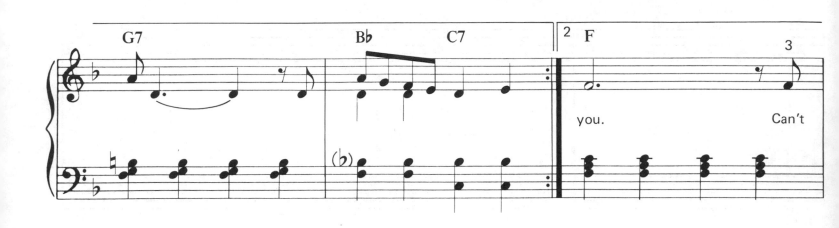

you. Can't

help my - self, I fall in love with you.

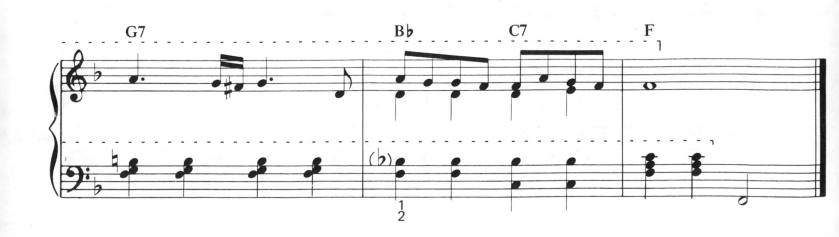

I LOVE YOU

Words and Music by
COLE PORTER

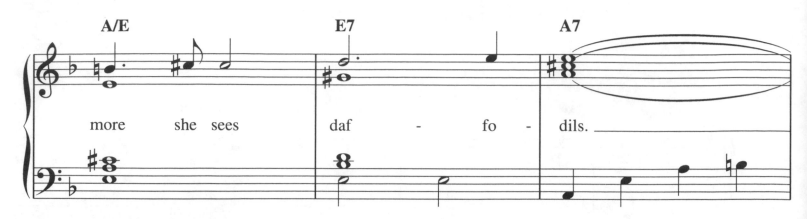

more she sees daf - fo - dils. _____

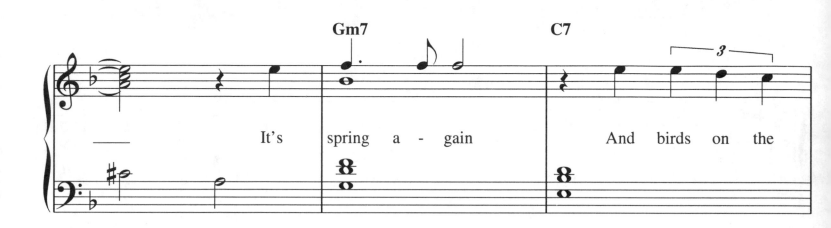

_____ It's spring a - gain And birds on the

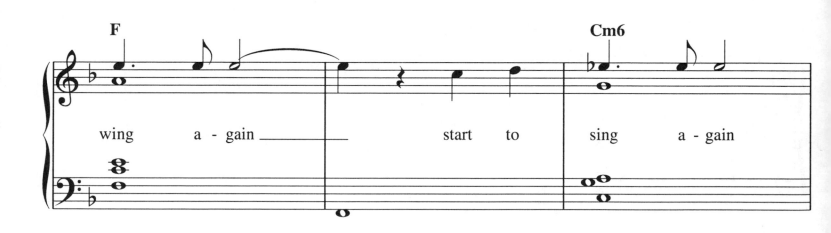

wing a - gain _____ start to sing a - gain

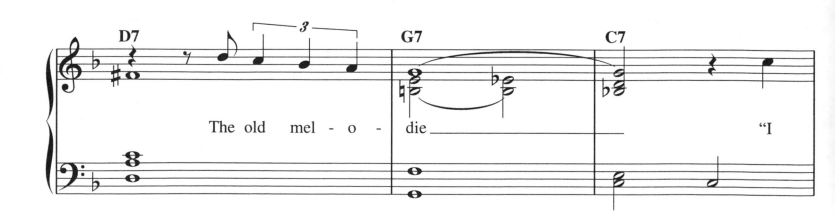

The old mel - o - die _____ "I

love you," That's the song of songs

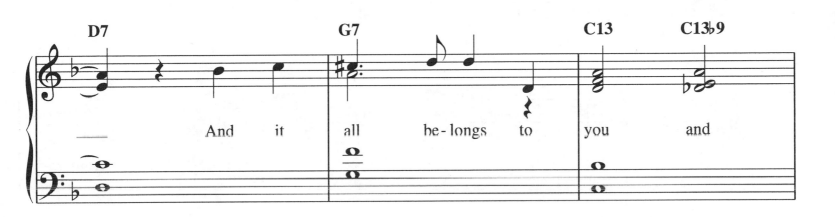

And it all be-longs to you and

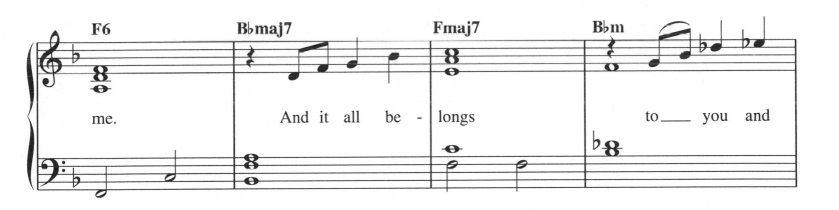

me. And it all be - longs to you and

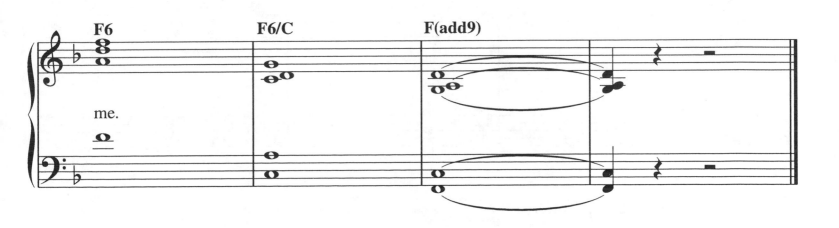

me.

I WANT YOU, I NEED YOU, I LOVE YOU

Words by MAURICE MYSELS
Music by IRA KOSLOFF

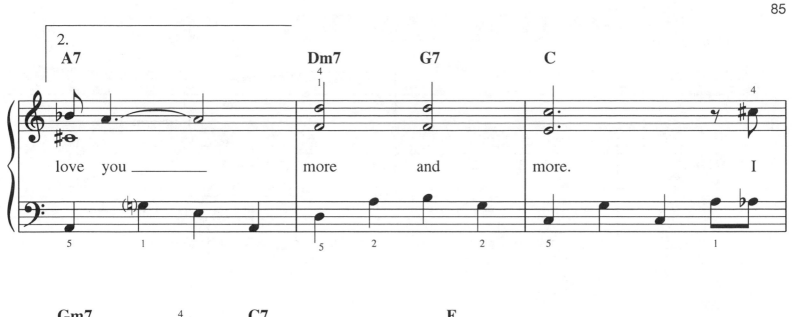

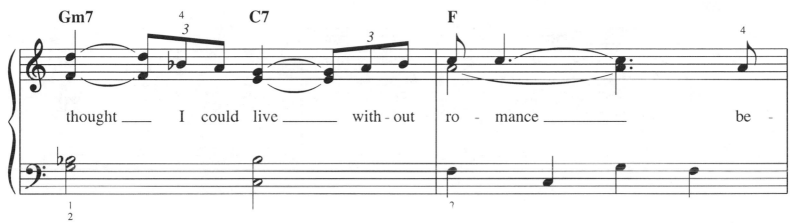

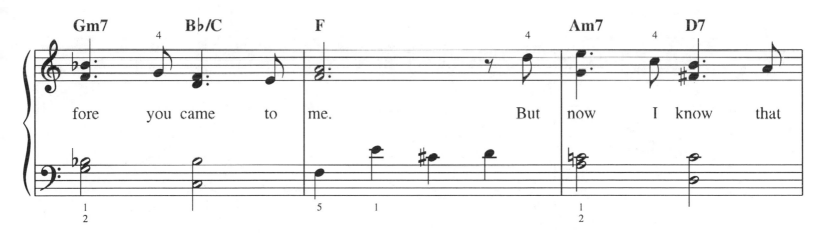

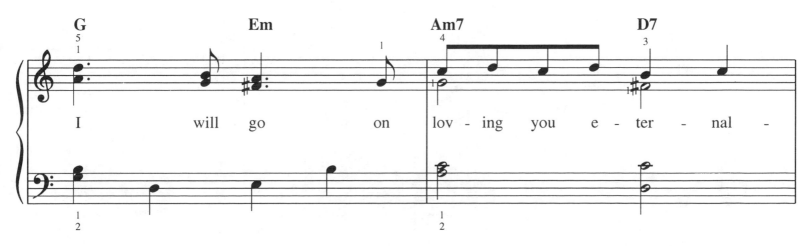

ly.   Won't you   please _____ be my   own? _____ Nev - er

leave _____ me a - lone, _____ 'Cause I   die _____ ev - 'ry time _____ we're a -

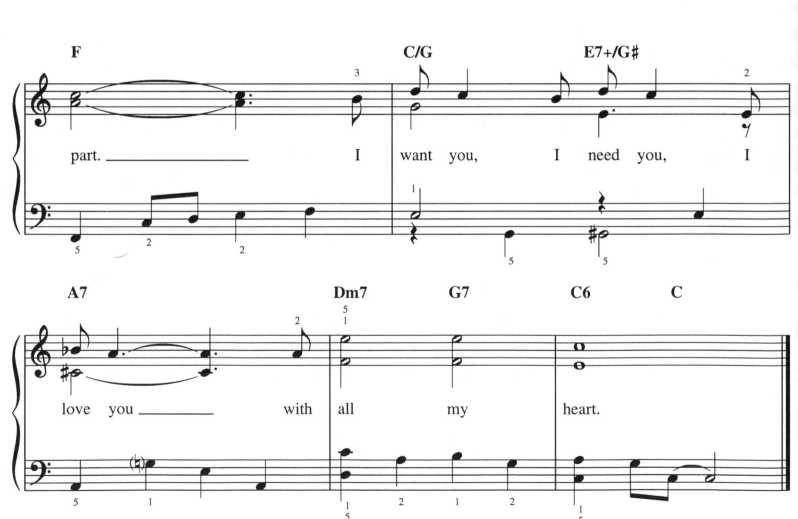

part. _____   I   want you,   I   need you,   I

love you _____ with   all   my   heart.

I.O.U.

Words and Music by KERRY CHATER
and AUSTIN ROBERTS

Moderately Slow Ballad

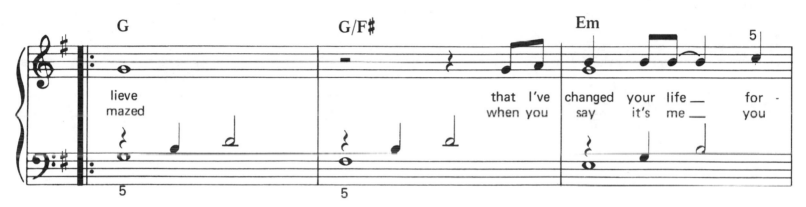

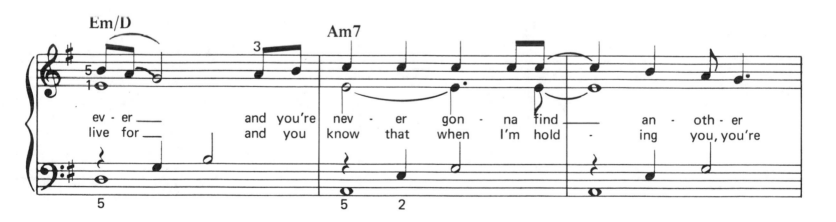

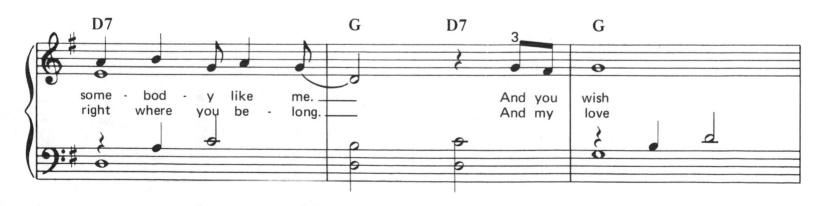

MCA music publishing

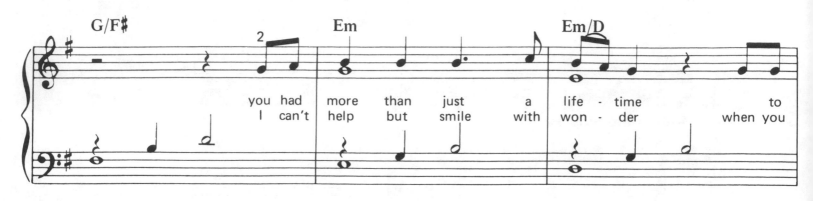

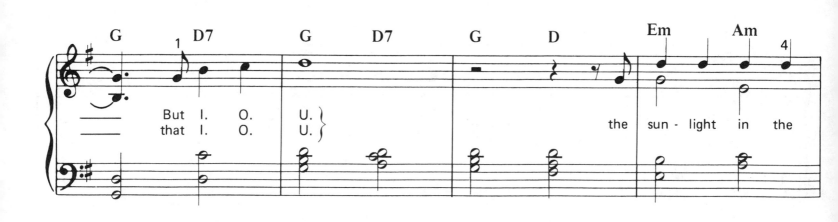

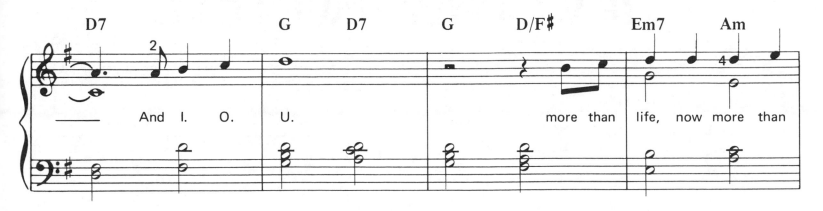

And I. O. U. _____ more than life, now more than

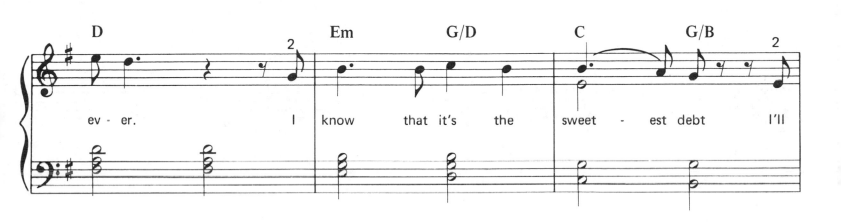

ev - er. I know that it's the sweet - est debt I'll

ev - er have to pay. _____

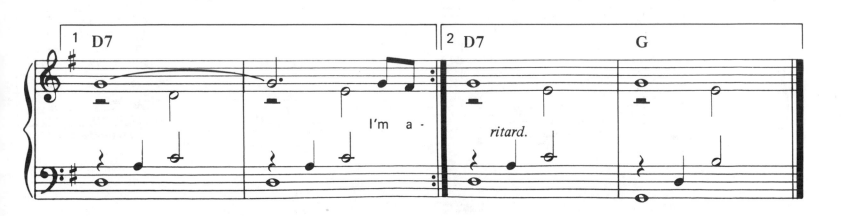

I'm a - *ritard.*

IF WE ONLY HAVE LOVE

English Lyrics by MORT SHUMAN and ERIC BLAU
Original French Lyrics and Music by JACQUES BREL

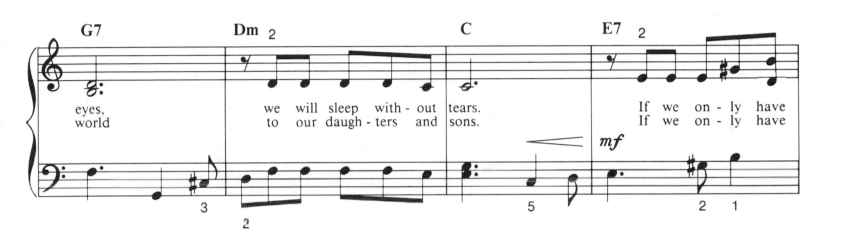

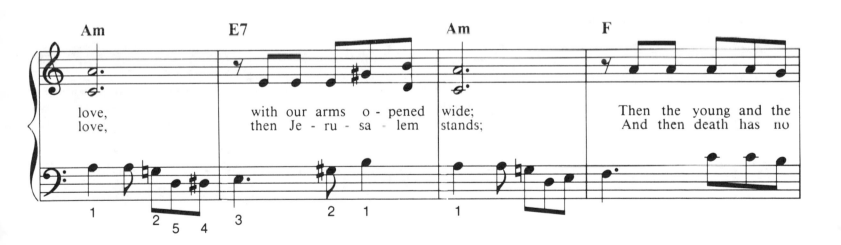

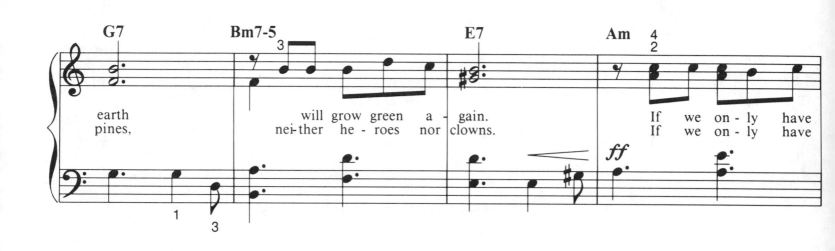

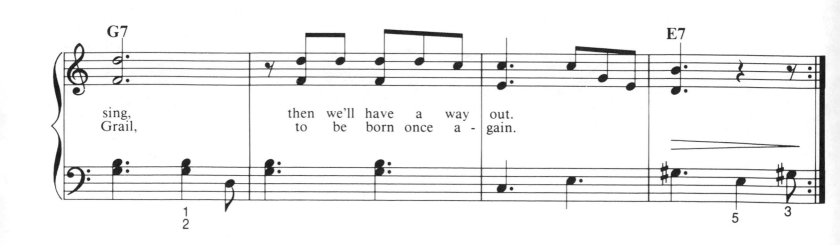

93

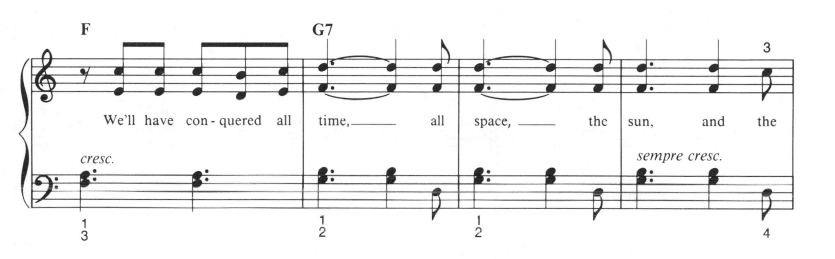

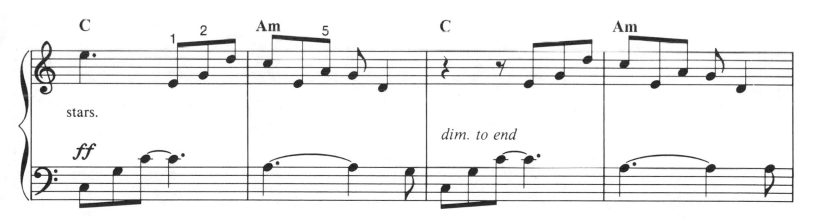

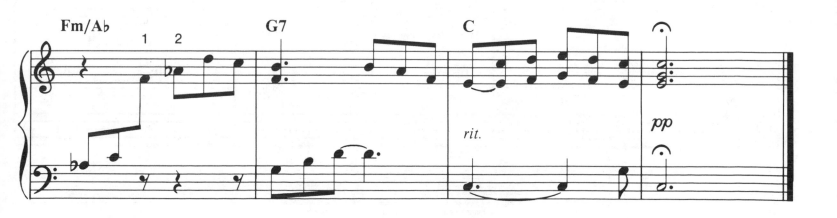

IF YOU REMEMBER ME

Words by CAROLE BAYER SAGER
Music by MARVIN HAMLISCH

with you now, but where - ev - er you go _____

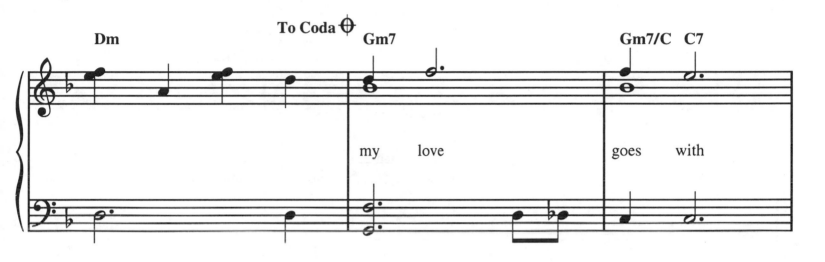

To Coda ⊕

my love goes with

you. Keep on
I'll be

smil - ing. Keep on shin - ing
with you. Keep be - liev - ing.

ISN'T IT ROMANTIC?
from the Paramount Picture LOVE ME TONIGHT

Words by LORENZ HART
Music by RICHARD RODGERS

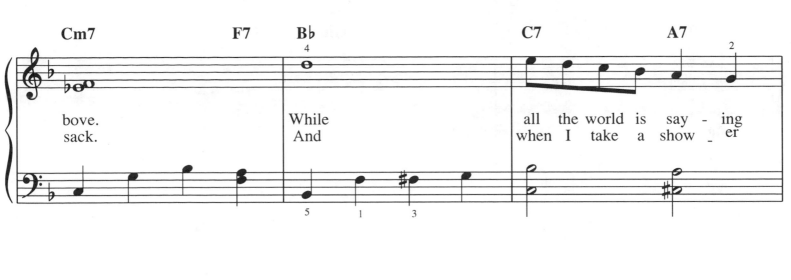

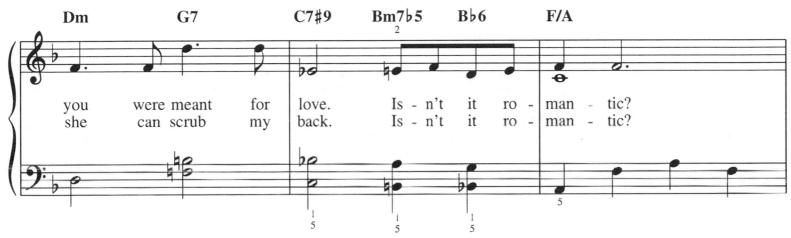

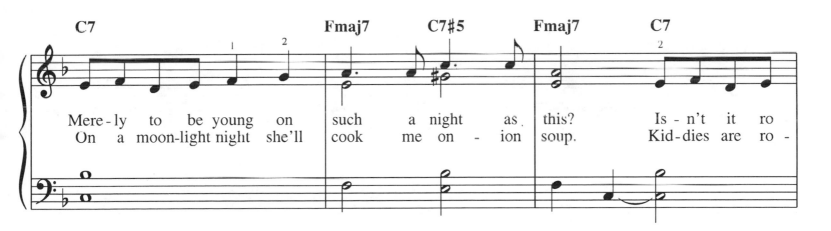

100

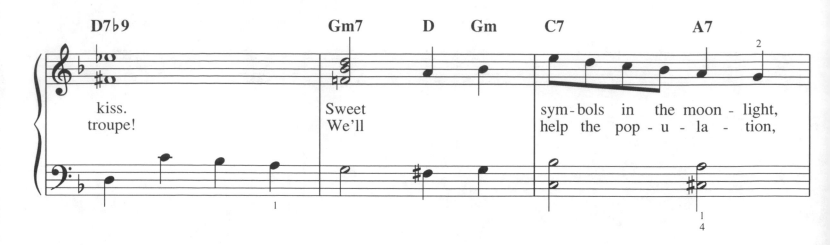

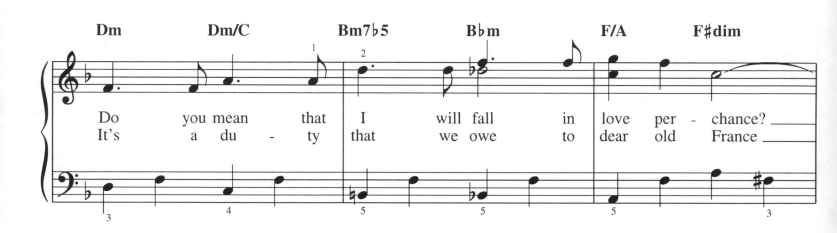

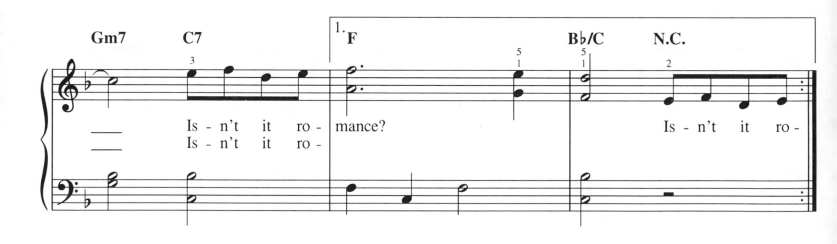

JUST THE WAY YOU ARE

Words and Music by
BILLY JOEL

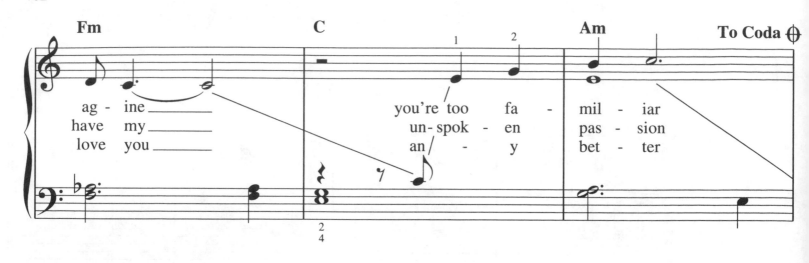

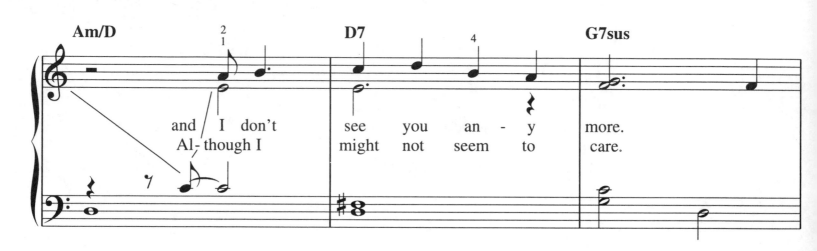

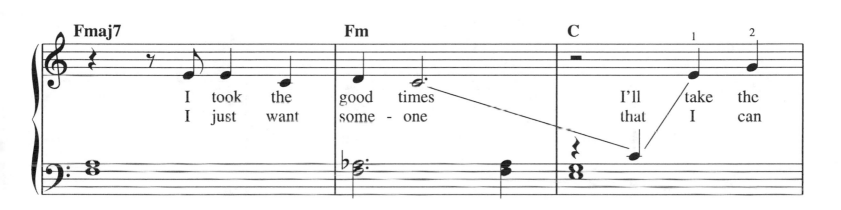

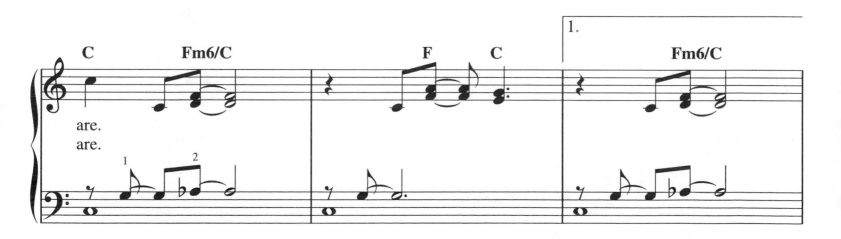

I need to know that you will al - ways

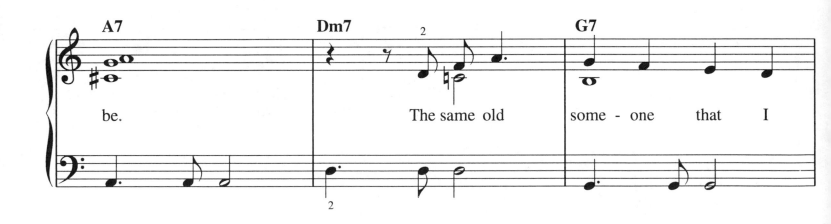

be. The same old some - one that I

knew. Oh! What will it

take till you be - lieve in me

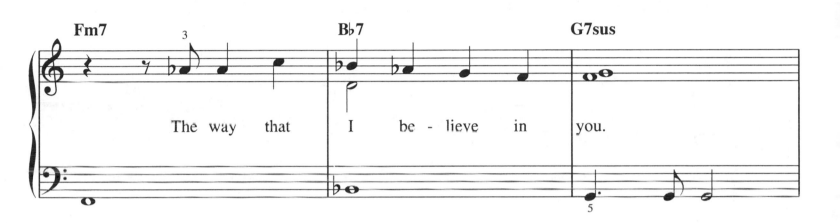

The way that I be - lieve in you.

I

I want you just the way you

are.

THE LAST TIME I FELT LIKE THIS

from SAME TIME, NEXT YEAR

Words by ALAN BERGMAN and MARILYN BERGMAN
Music by MARVIN HAMLISCH

Slow Ballad Tempo

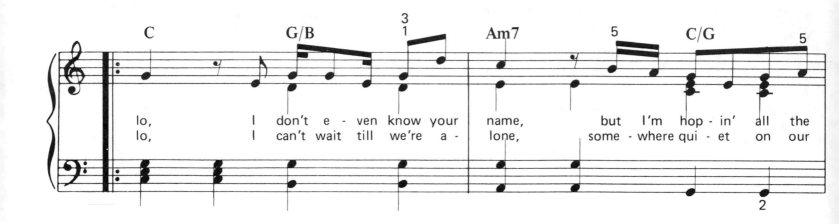

lo, I don't e - ven know your name, but I'm hop - in' all the

lo, I can't wait till we're a - lone, some - where qui - et on our

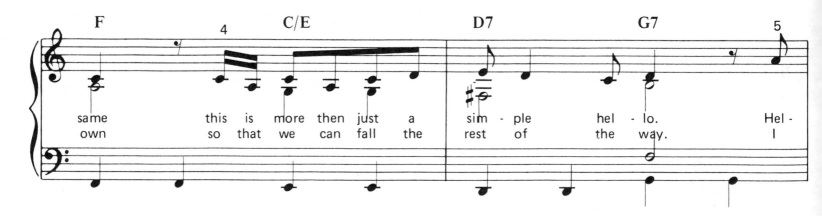

same this is more then just a sim - ple hel - lo. Hel -

own so that we can fall the rest of the way. I

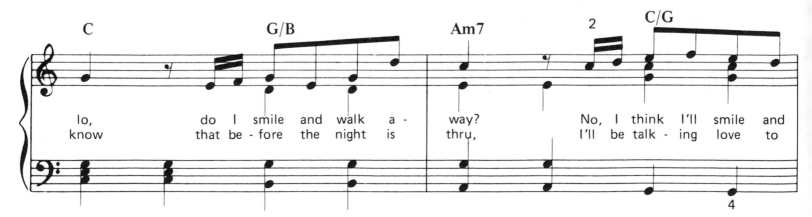

lo, do I smile and walk a - way? No, I think I'll smile and

know that be - fore the night is thru, I'll be talk - ing love to

MCA music publishing

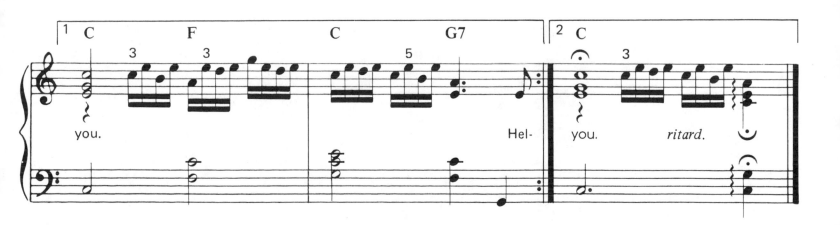

LET IT BE ME

(Je T'appartiens)

English Words by MANN CURTIS
French Words by PIERRE DeLANOE
Music by GILBERT BECAUD

In a relaxed tempo

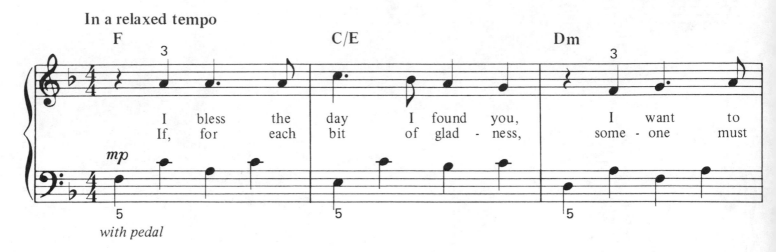

I bless the day I found you,
If, for each bit of glad - ness,
I want to some - one to must

stay a - round you,
taste of sad - ness,
And so I
I'll bear the
beg you,
sor - row,

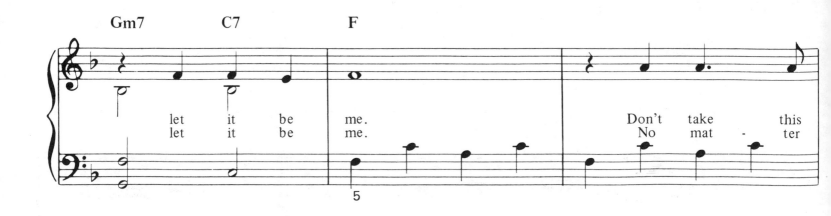

let it be me.
let it be me.
Don't take this
No mat - ter

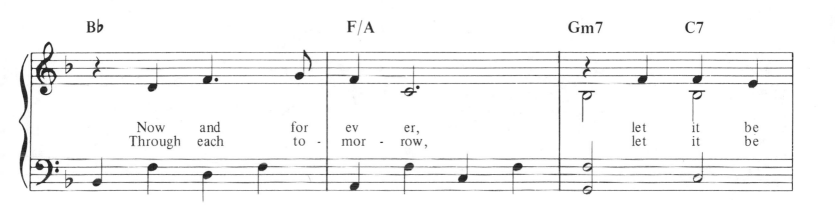

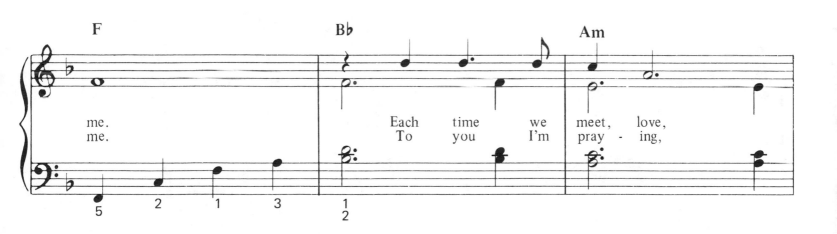

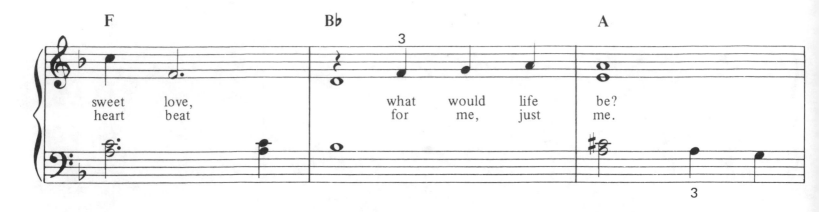

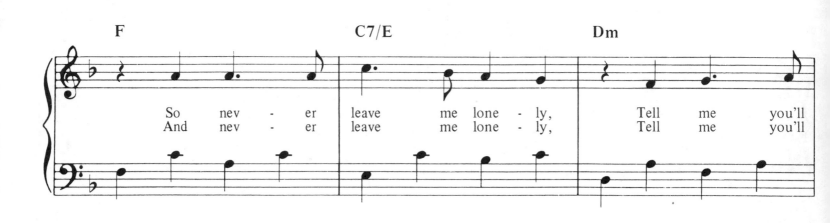

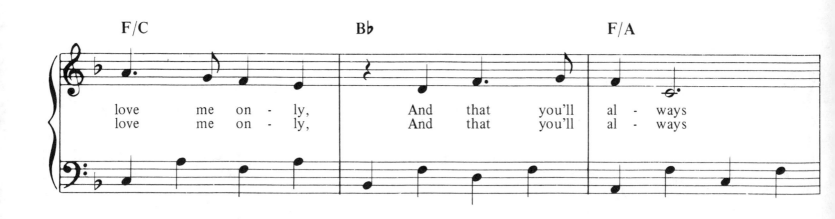

LONG AGO
(And Far Away)
from COVER GIRL

Words by IRA GERSHWIN
Music by JEROME KERN

LONGER

Words and Music by
DAN FOGELBERG

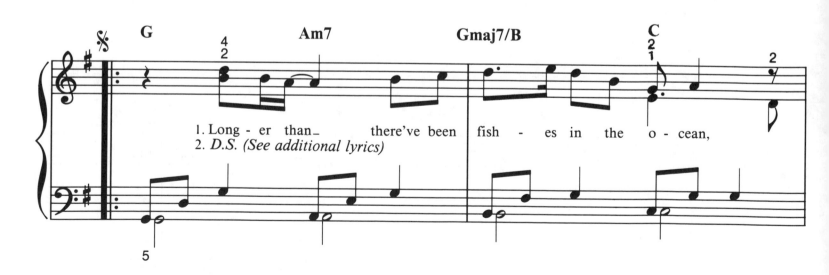

1. Long - er than_____ there've been fish - es in the o - cean,
2. D.S. (See additional lyrics)

116

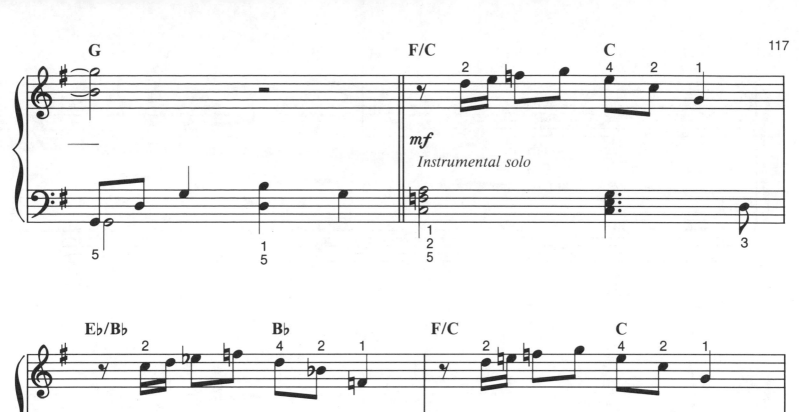

mf

Instrumental solo

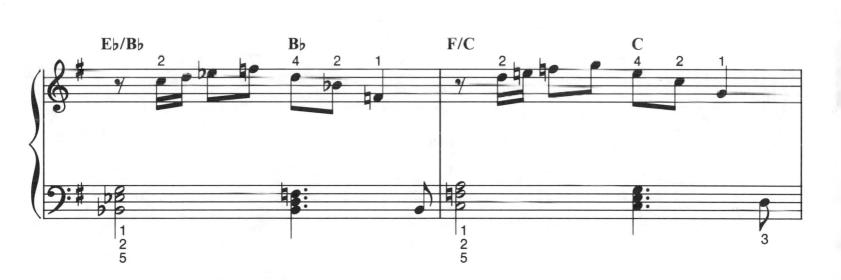

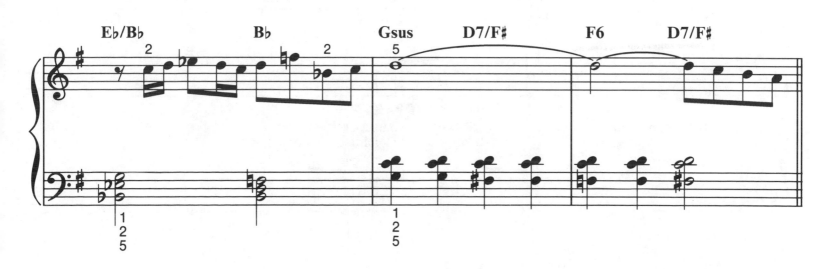

I am in love____ with you.____

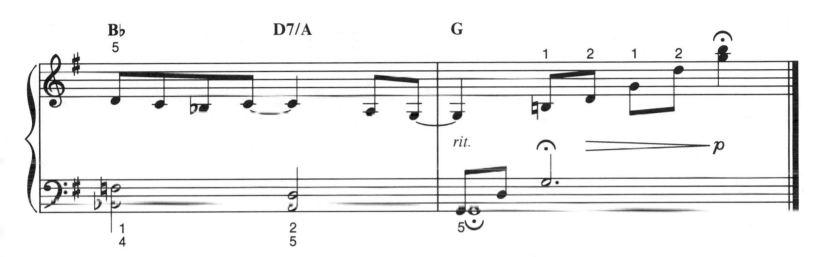

rit.

Additional Lyrics

2. Stronger than any mountain cathedral,
Truer than any tree ever grew,
Deeper than any forest primeval,
I am in love with you.

(I'll bring . . . etc.)

D.S. Through the years as the fire starts mellow,
Burning lines in the book of our lives.
Though the binding cracks and the pages start to yellow,
I'll be in love with you.

(I'll be in love with you. INSTRUMENTAL SOLO)

LOST IN YOUR EYES

Words and Music by
DEBORAH GIBSON

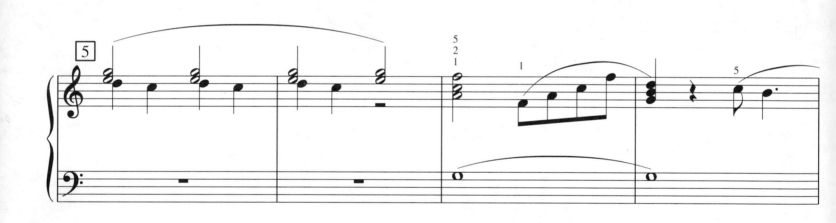

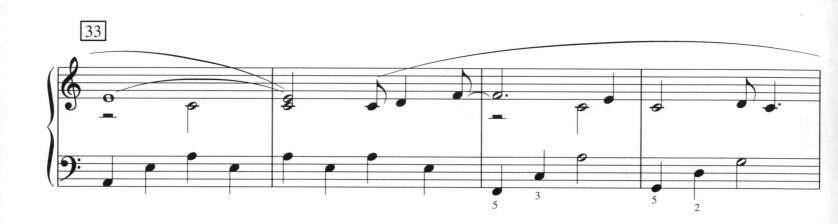

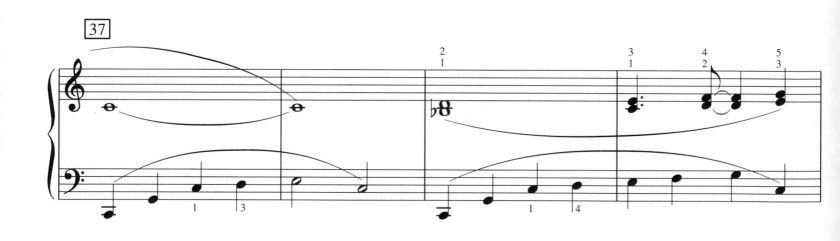

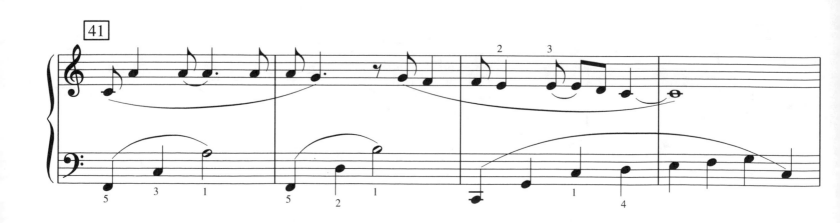

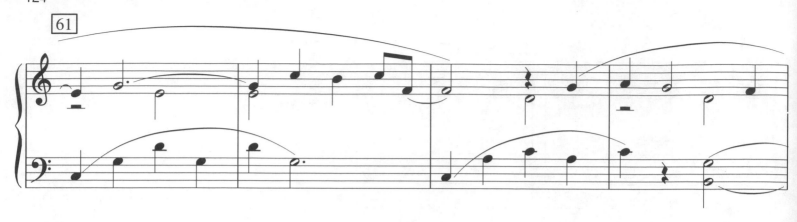

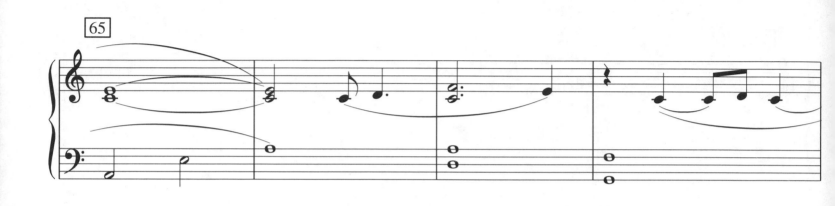

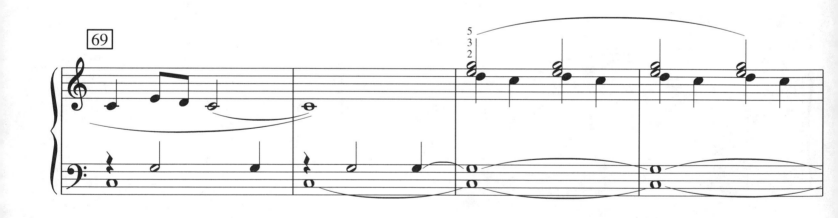

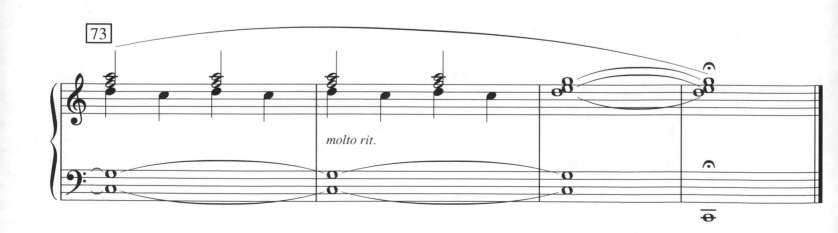

molto rit.

LOVE IS HERE TO STAY

from GOLDWYN FOLLIES

Music and Lyrics by GEORGE GERSHWIN
and IRA GERSHWIN

With pedal

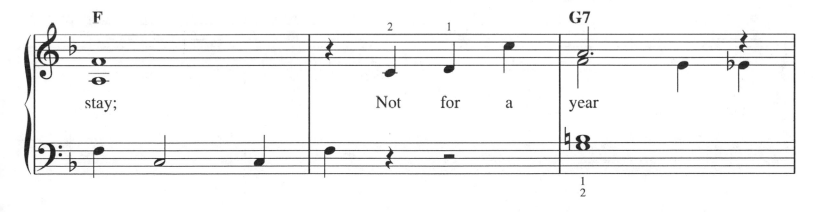

It's ver - y clear   Our love is here to

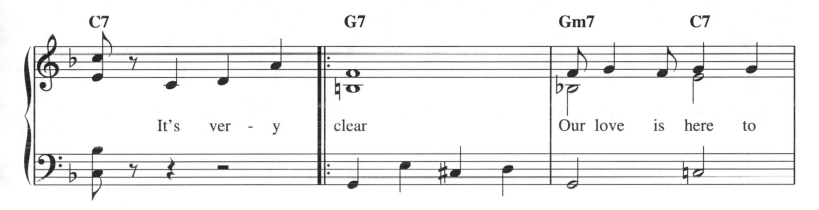

stay;   Not for a year   The ra - di -

But ev - er and a day.   The ra - di -

126

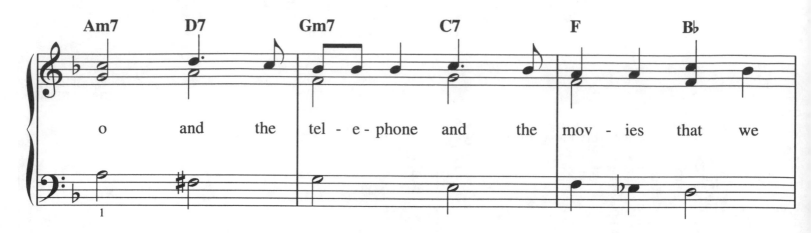

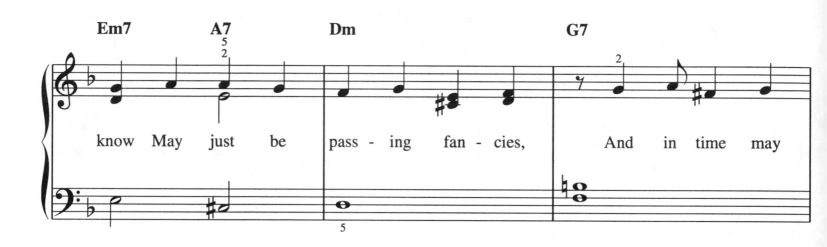

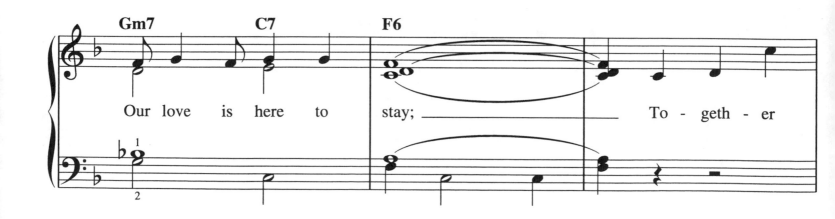

LOVE ME TENDER

Words and Music by ELVIS PRESLEY
and VERA MATSON

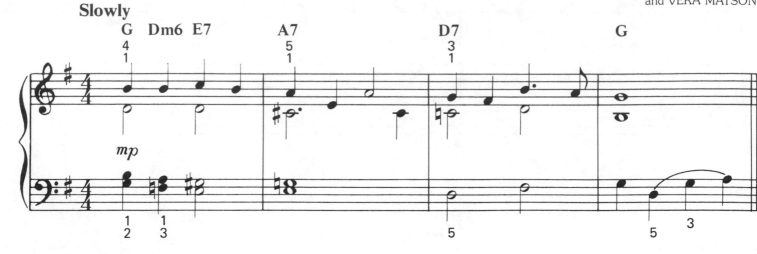

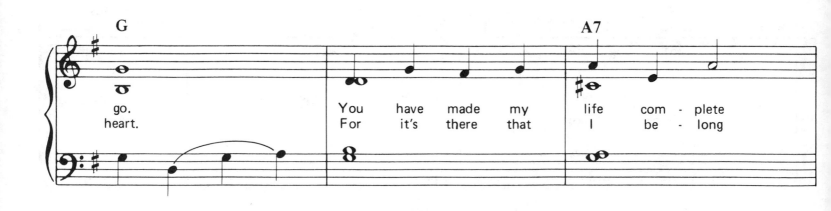

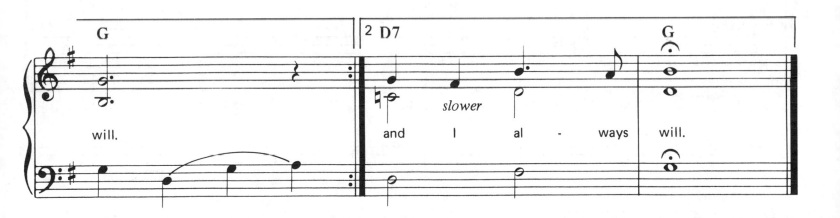

3. Love me tender, love me dear,
   Tell me you are mine.
   I'll be yours through all the years
   "Till the end of time."

4. When at last my dreams come true,
   Darling, this I know:
   Happiness will follow you
   Everywhere you go.

A LOVE SONG

Words and Music by
LEE GREENWOOD

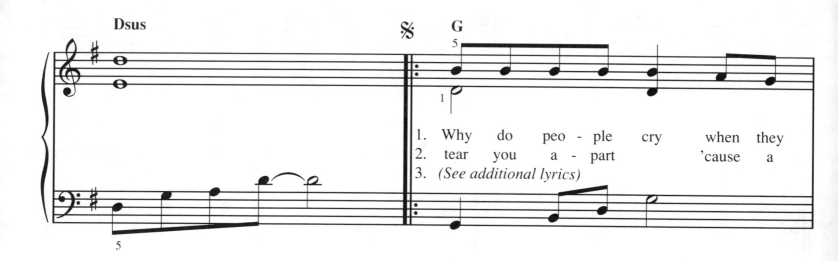

1. Why do peo - ple cry when they
2. tear you a - part 'cause a
3. *(See additional lyrics)*

hear the word good - bye in a love song? __
word can break a heart in a love song. __

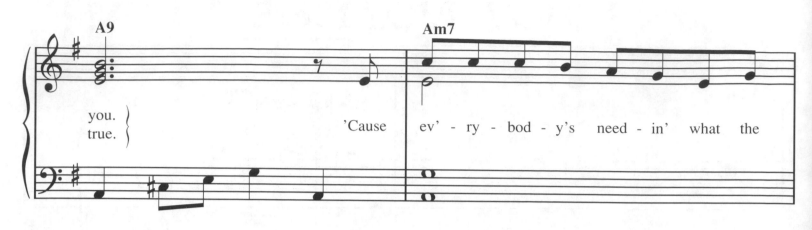

you.
true.

'Cause ev'-ry-bod-y's need-in' what the

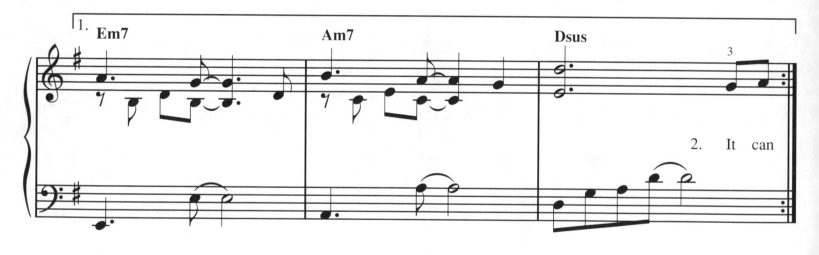

sing-ers all are sing-in' in a love song. _____

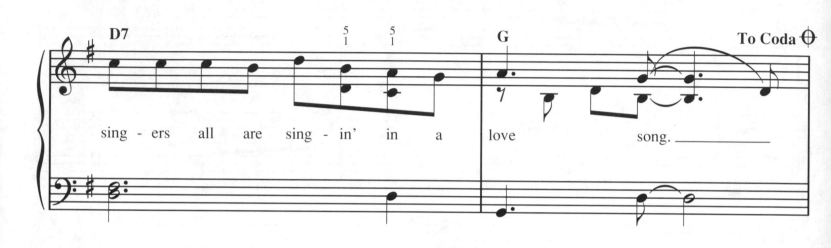

2. It can

Each of us know __ there's no guar-an-tee __ we'll

ev - er find love. _____ And in the songs that we share _ the

heart-ache is there _ to re - mind us. ___

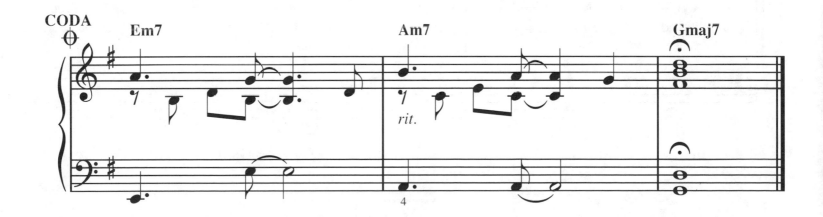

Additional Lyrics

3. New love brings a thrill and we know it always will
   In a love song.
   Happiness can leave but it helps if we believe
   In a love song.
   There's a part of you and me in ev'ry memory
   That tells us who we are.

LOVE TAKES TIME

Words and Music by MARIAH CAREY
and BEN MARGULIES

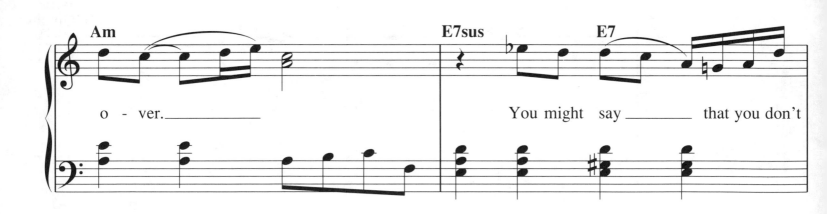

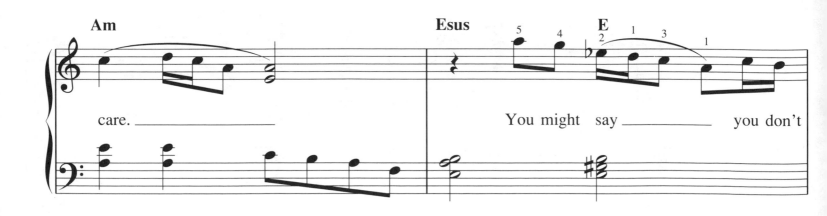

miss me, you don't need ___ me. But I know that you do and I feel that you do in-

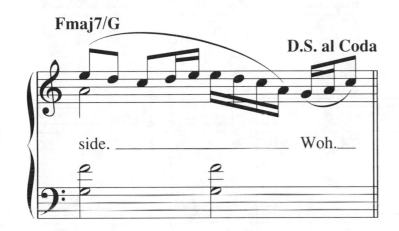

side. _____ Woh.___

D.S. al Coda

CODA

I don't want to be there.

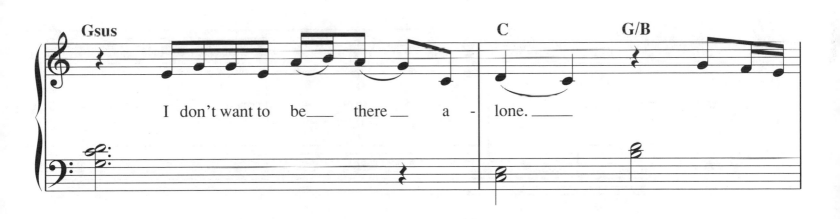

I don't want to be___ there___ a - lone.___

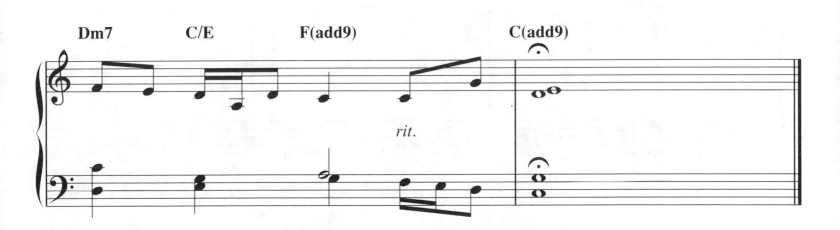

rit.

LOVING YOU

Words and Music by JERRY LEIBER
and MIKE STOLLER

139

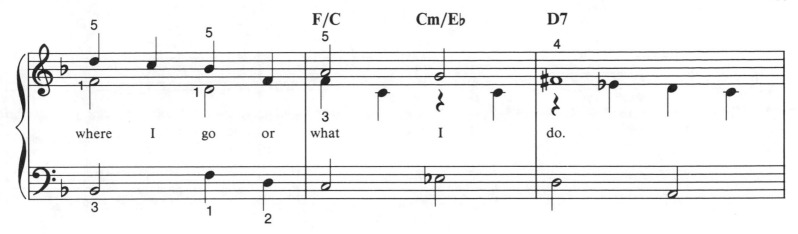

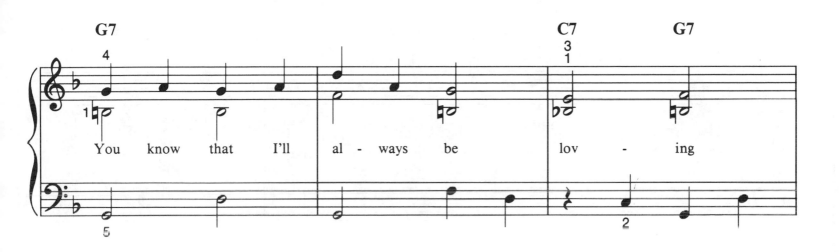

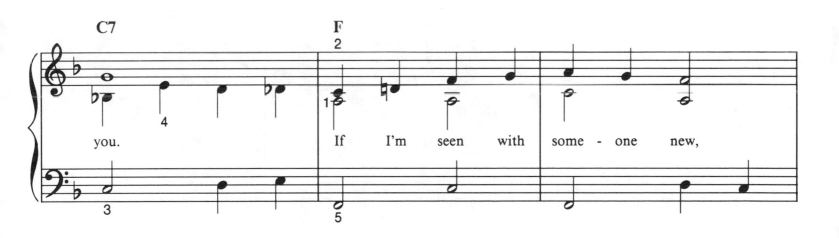

I'll be true, al - ways true, — true to you. —

There is on - ly one for me, and you know

who. You know that I'll al - ways be

lov - ing you. you.

MY FUNNY VALENTINE

from BABES IN ARMS

Words by LORENZ HART
Music by RICHARD RODGERS

Slowly

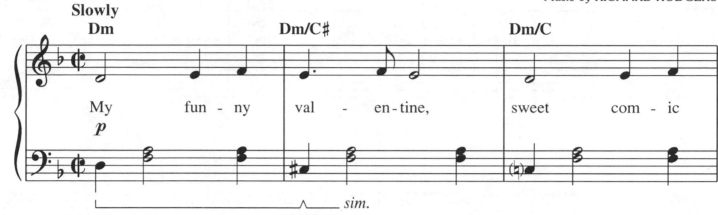

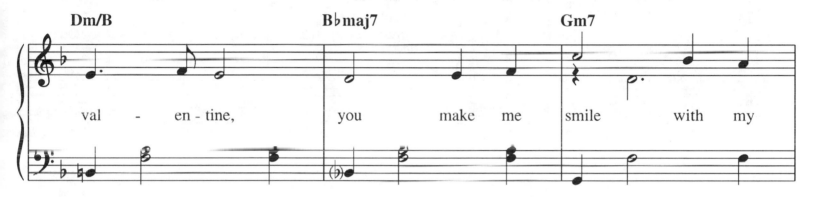

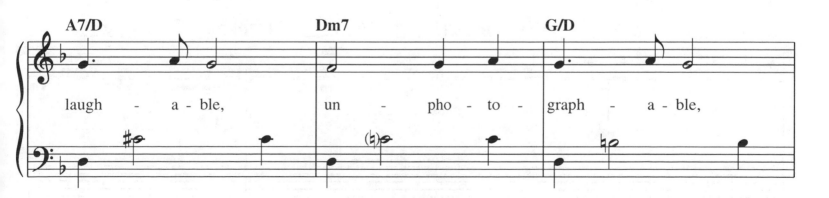

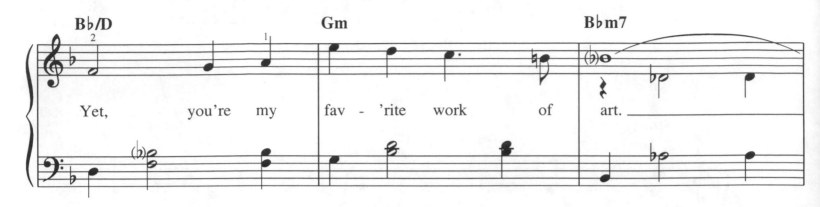

Yet, you're my fav - 'rite work of art. _____

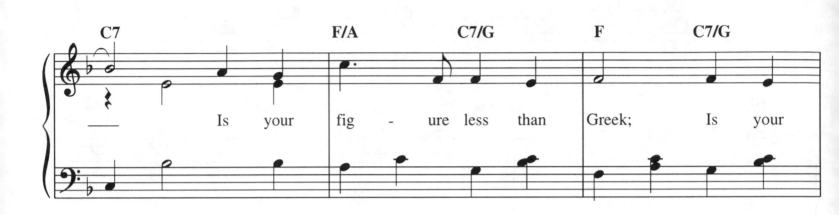

_____ Is your fig - ure less than Greek; Is your

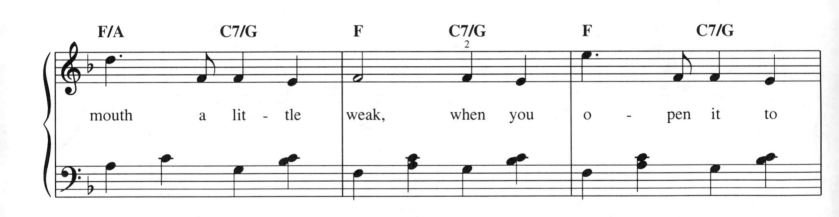

mouth a lit - tle weak, when you o - pen it to

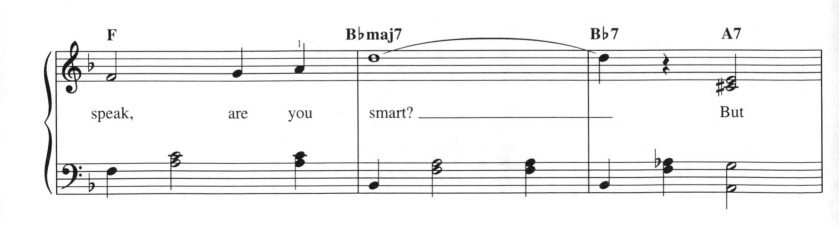

speak, are you smart? _____ But

143

don't change a hair for me, not if you

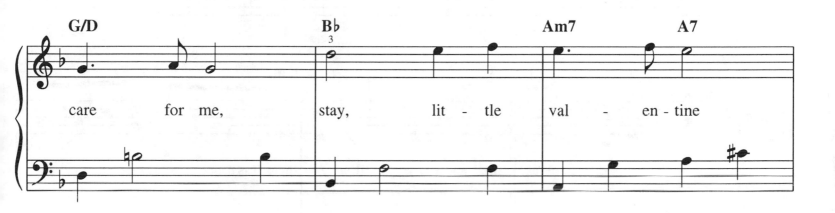

care for me, stay, lit - tle val - en - tine

stay! _____ Each day is

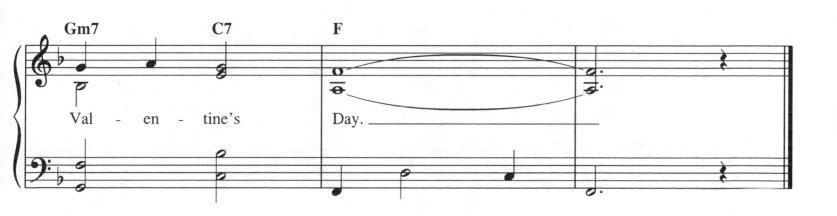

Val - en - tine's Day. _____

MISTY

Words by JOHNNY BURKE
Music by ERROLL GARNER

145

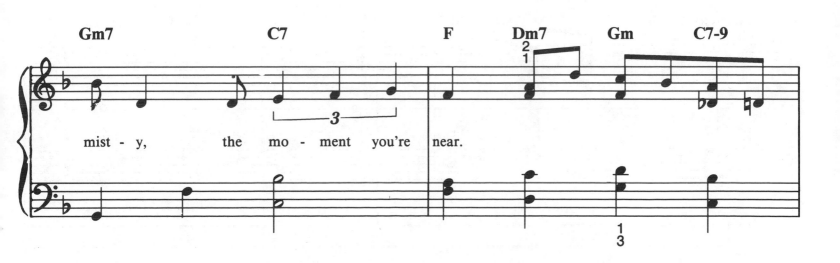

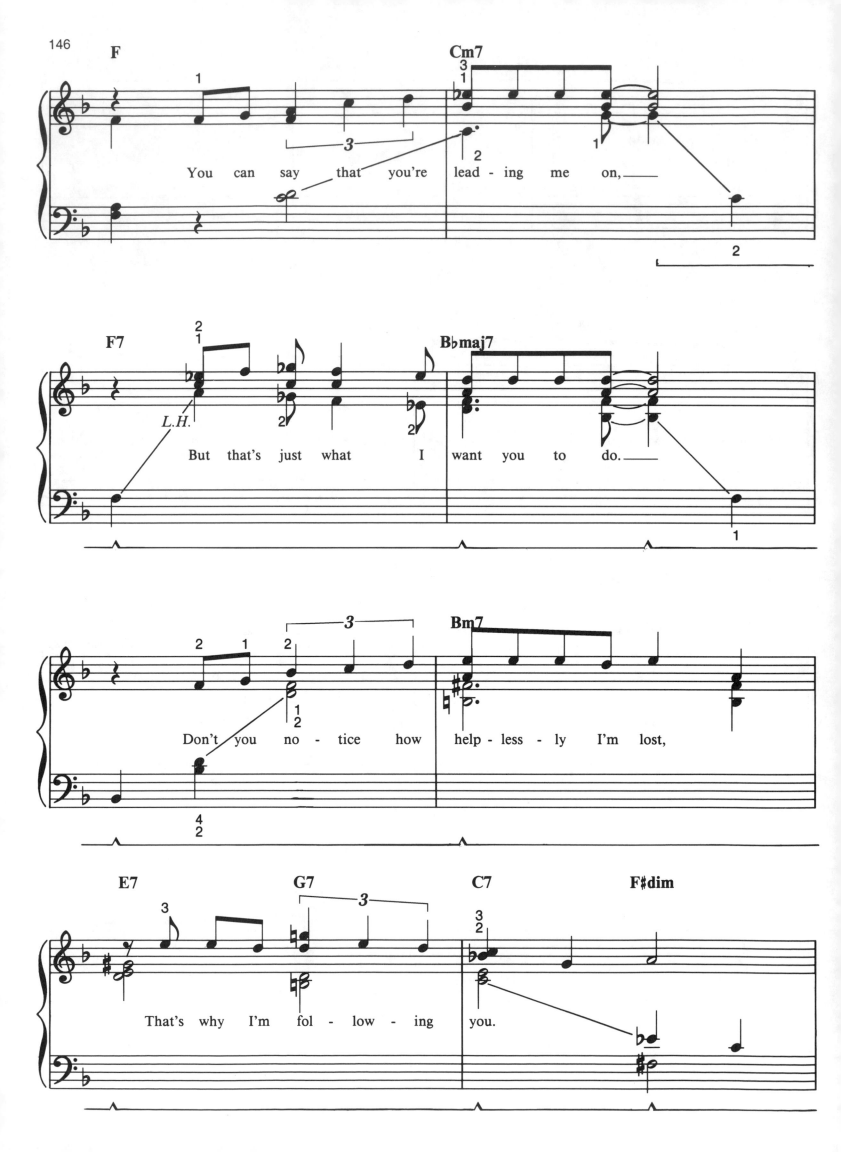

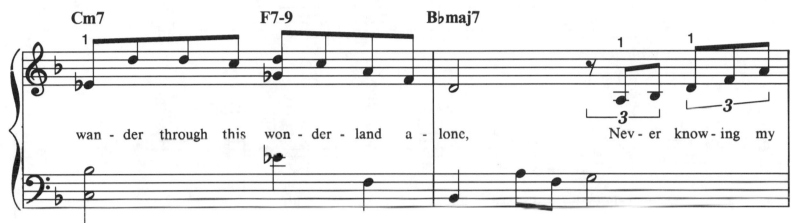

P.S. I LOVE YOU

Words by JOHNNY MERCER
Music by GORDON JENKINS

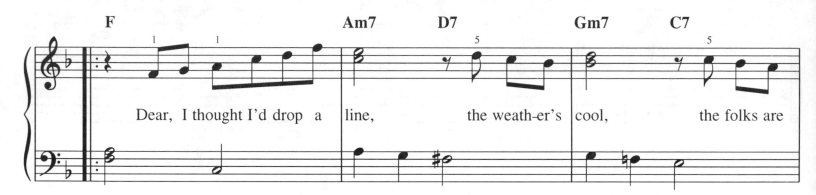

Dear, I thought I'd drop a line, the weath-er's cool, the folks are

fine. I'm in bed each night at nine,

P. S. I love you. Yes-ter-day we had some

MCA music publishing

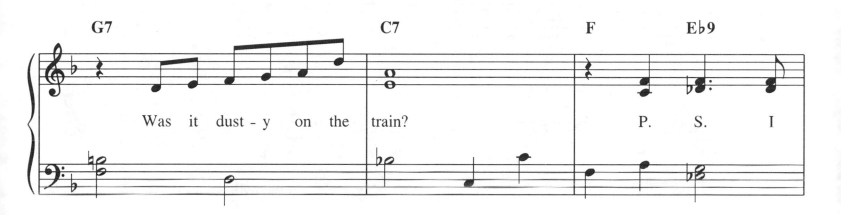

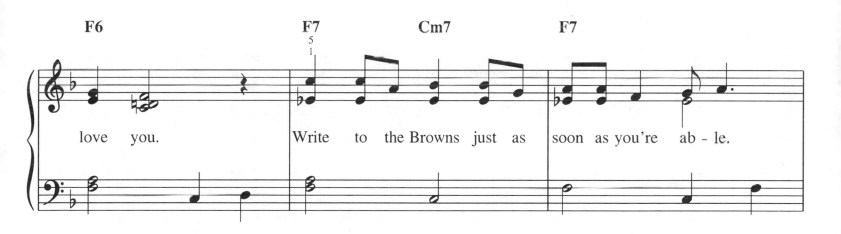

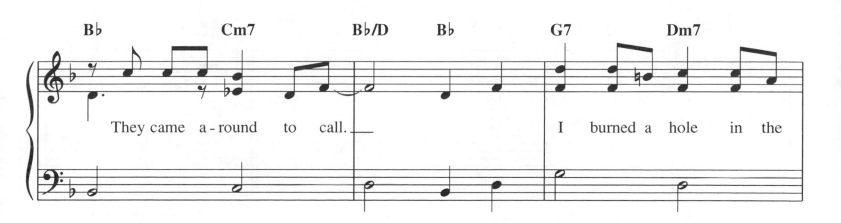

din - ing room ta - ble. And let me see, I guess that's all. ___

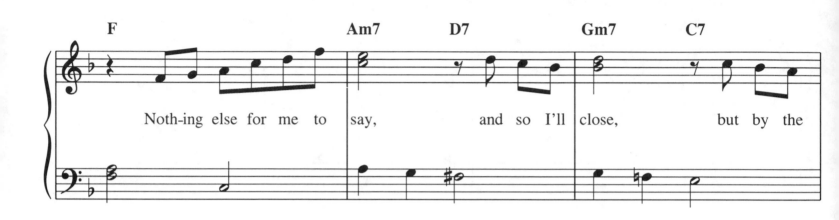

Noth-ing else for me to say, and so I'll close, but by the

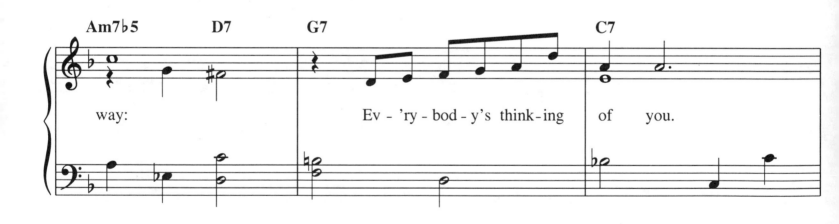

way: Ev - 'ry - bod - y's think-ing of you.

P. S. I love you.

love you. ___

SEA OF LOVE

Words and Music by GEORGE KHOURY
and PHILIP BAPTISTE

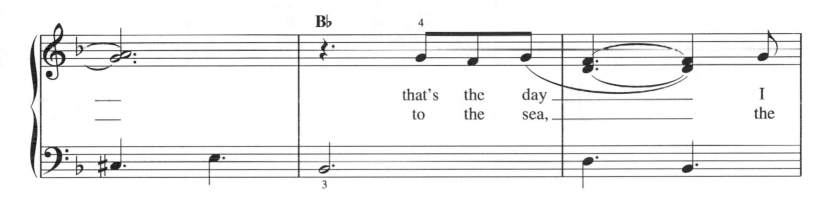

love   you. ___

To Coda ⊕ F

1.

2. F

Come _____ with   me _____

C   B♭

to _____ the   sea _____

C   B♭

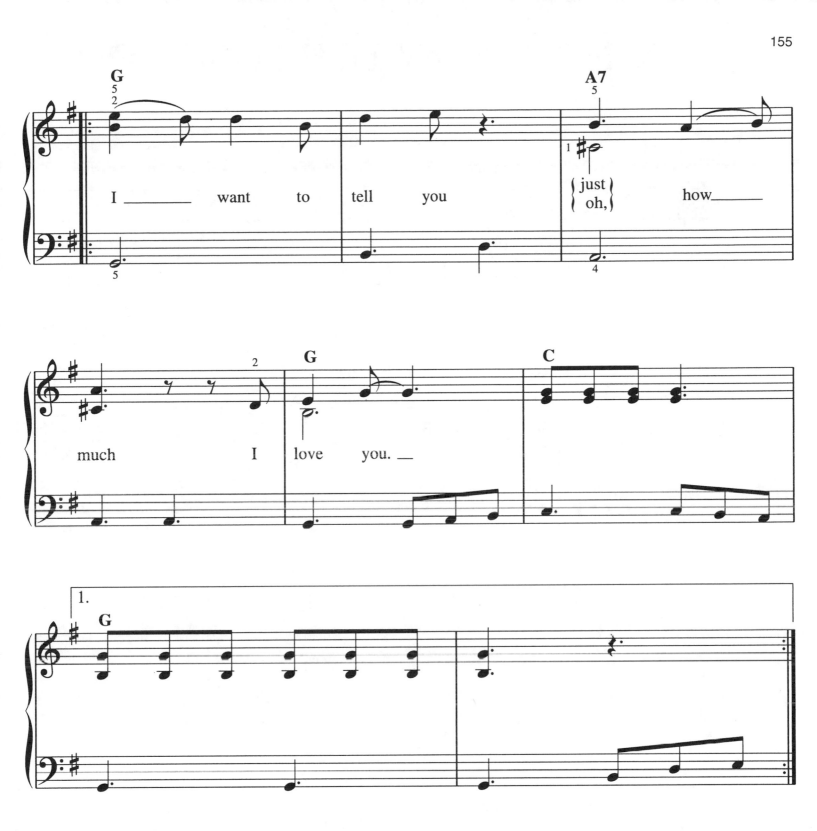

I _____ want to tell you { just / oh, } how_____

much I love you. __

1.

2.

rit.

8va ---- ⌐

SAVING ALL MY LOVE FOR YOU

Words by GERRY GOFFIN
Music by MICHAEL MASSER

157

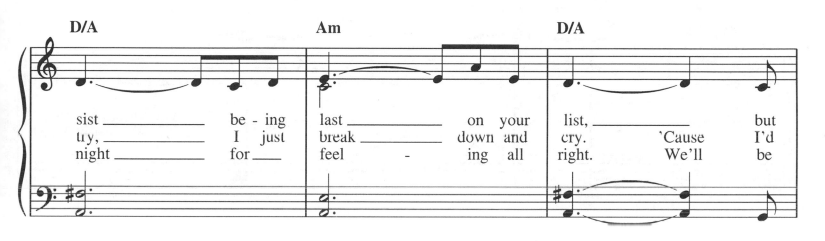

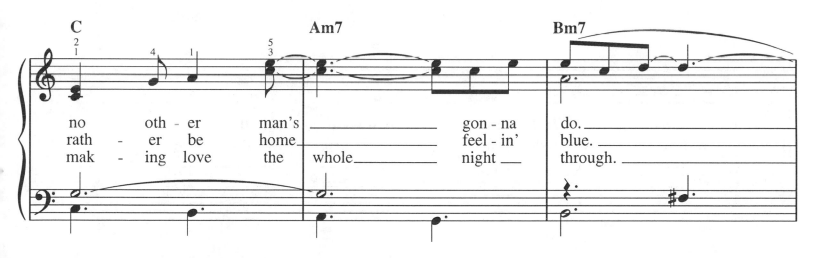

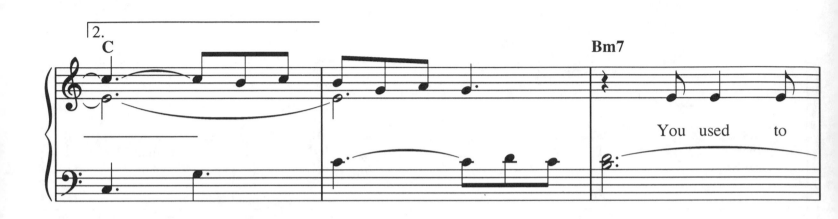

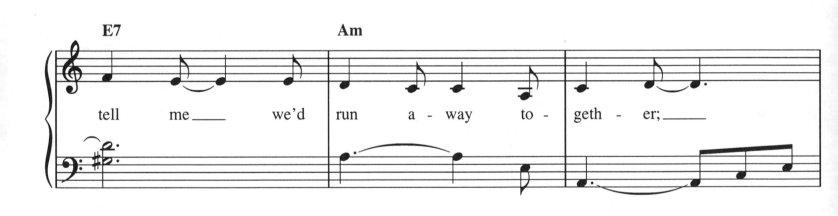

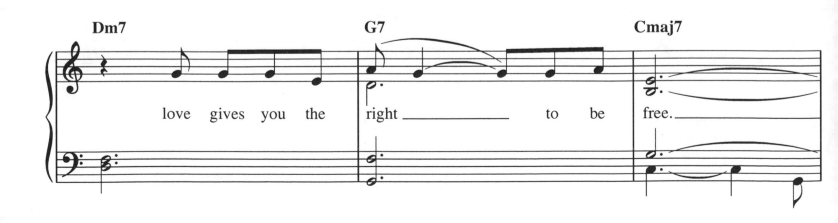

159

You said, _____ "Be pa - tient,_ just

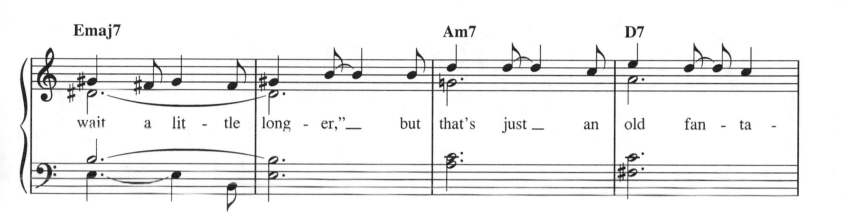

wait a lit - tle long - er,"_ but that's just_ an old fan - ta -

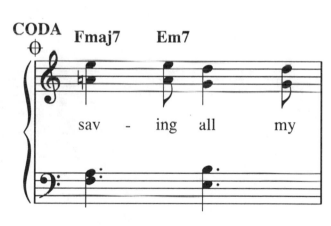

sy. _____ I've

sav - ing all my

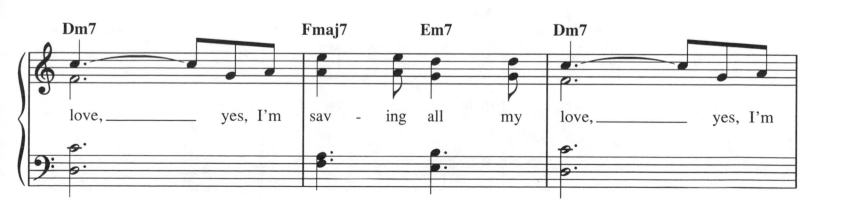

love, _____ yes, I'm sav - ing all my love, _____ yes, I'm

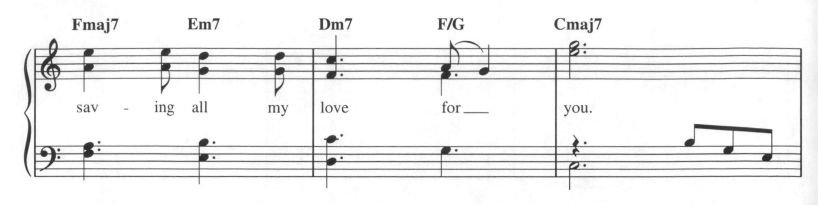

sav - ing all my love for ___ you.

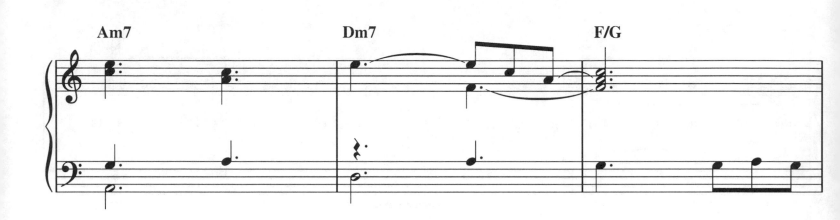

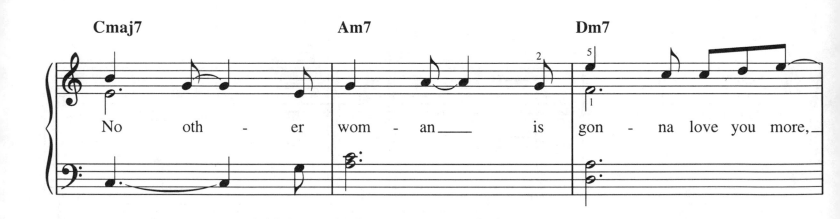

No oth - er wom - an ___ is gon - na love you more,

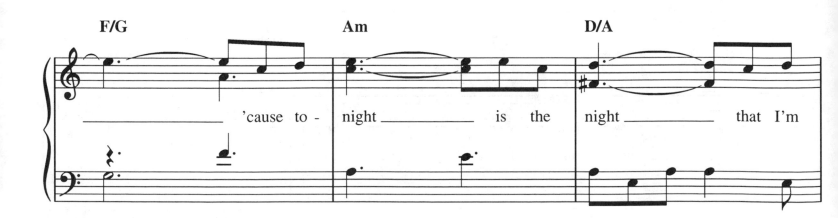

___ 'cause to - night ___ is the night ___ that I'm

feel - ing all right._____ We'll be mak - ing love the whole_____ night_____

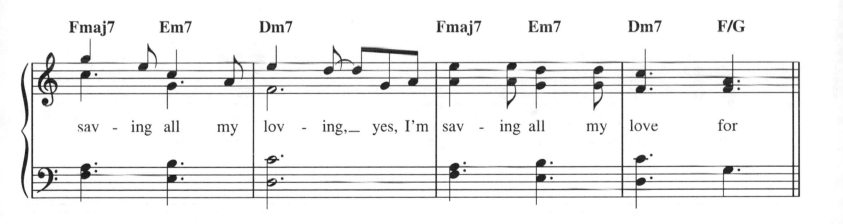

through._____ So I'm sav - ing all my love, yes, I'm

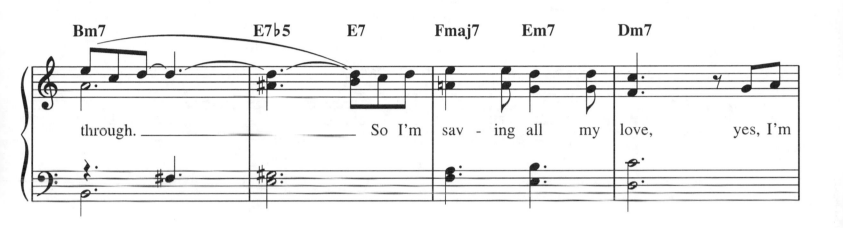

sav - ing all my lov - ing,__ yes, I'm sav - ing all my love for

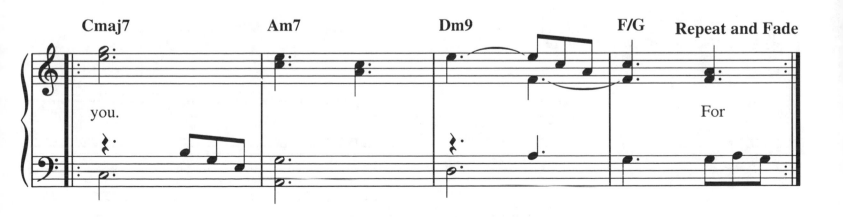

you. For

SEPTEMBER MORN

Words and Music by NEIL DIAMOND
and GILBERT BECAUD

Slowly, with expression

SHE BELIEVES IN ME

Words and Music by
STEVE GIBB

dream-ing __ I | try to get un-dressed __ with-out the | light. ____ Then

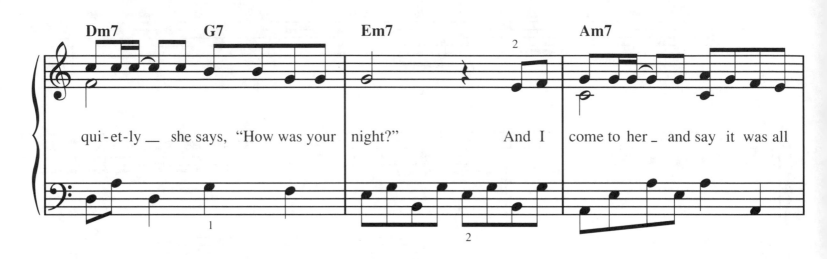

qui-et-ly __ she says, "How was your | night?" And I | come to her _ and say it was all

right. And I | hold her tight | And she be -

lieves in me. | I'll nev - er know just what she | sees in me.

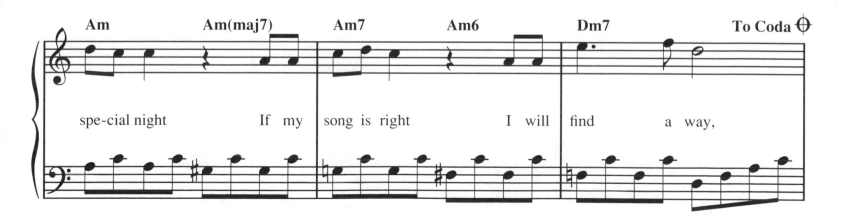

168

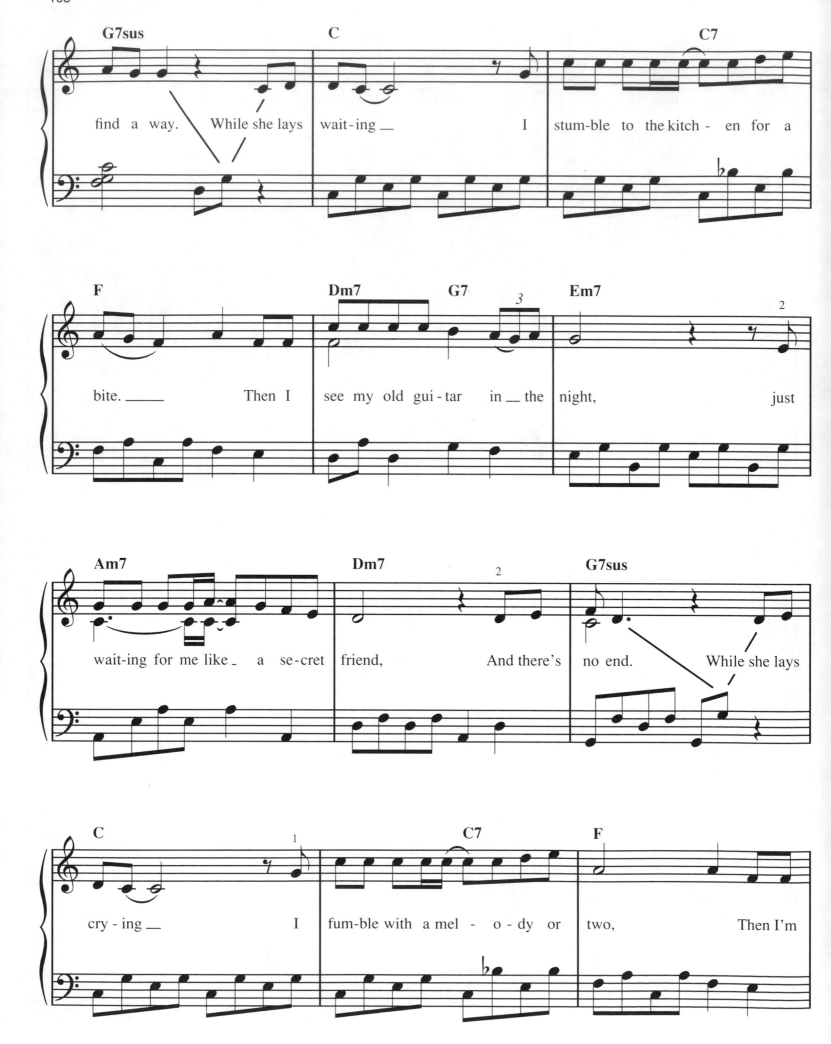

SHARE YOUR LOVE WITH ME

Words and Music by DEADRIC MALONE
and AL BRAGGS

MCA music publishing

share _____ your love with me. _____ It's a heart - ache

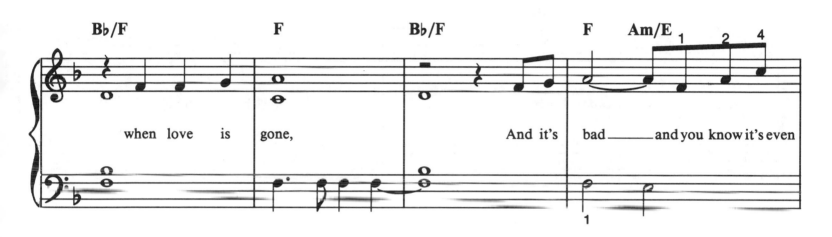

when love is gone, And it's bad _____ and you know it's even

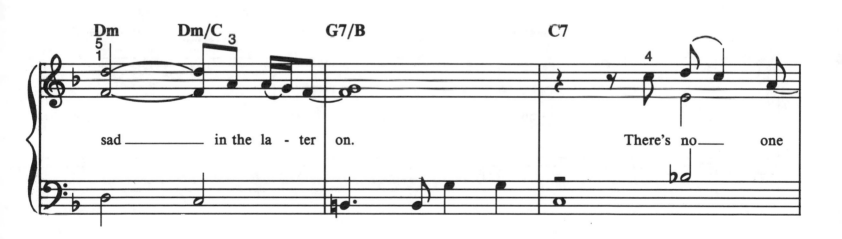

sad _____ in the la - ter on. There's no _____ one

blind - er than he who just won't see, And it's a

shame _____ if you don't share _____ your love with me. _____

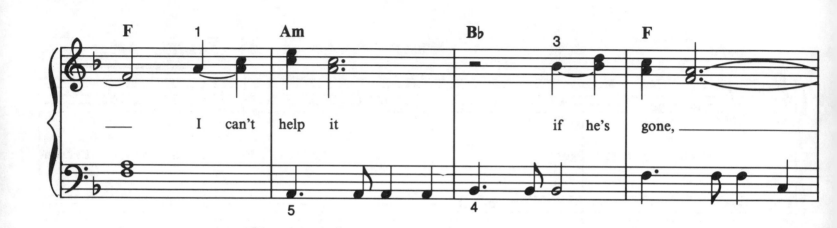

_____ I can't help it if he's gone, _____

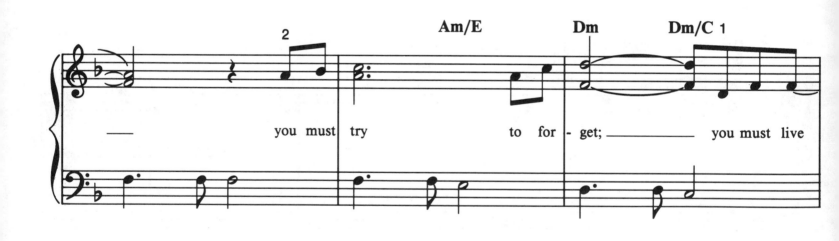

_____ you must try to for - get; _____ you must live

on. _____ Oh, how lone - some

SOME ENCHANTED EVENING

from SOUTH PACIFIC

Lyrics by OSCAR HAMMERSTEIN II
Music by RICHARD RODGERS

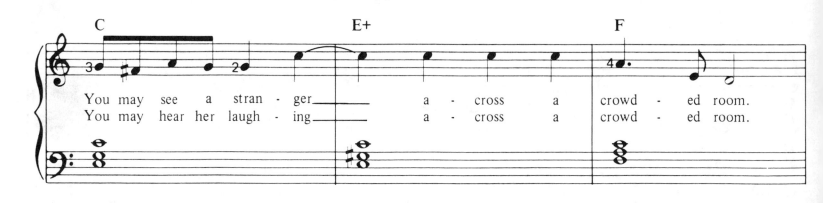

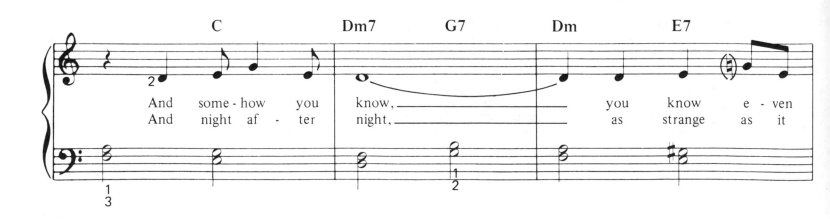

Am   C7/G   F   C/E   Dm

then_____ that some-where you'll see her a-
seems_____ the sound of her laugh-her will

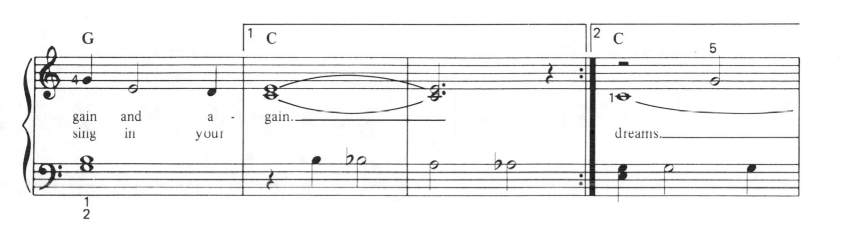

G   1 C   2 C

gain and a- gain._____
sing in your dreams._____

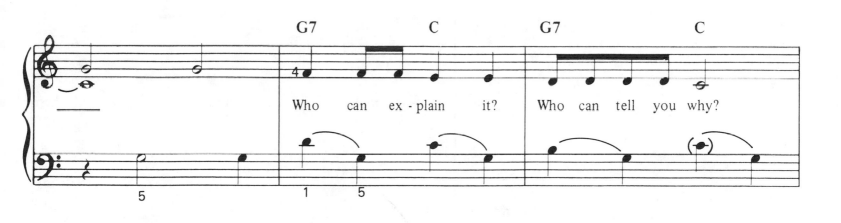

G7   C   G7   C

Who can ex-plain it? Who can tell you why?

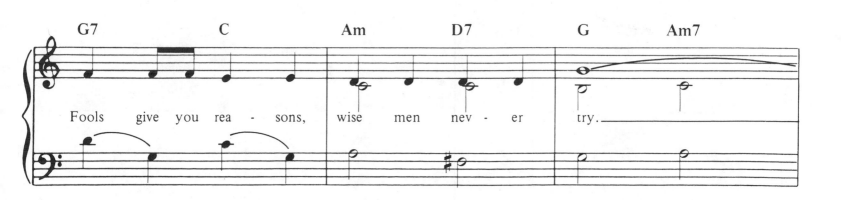

G7   C   Am   D7   G   Am7

Fools give you rea-sons, wise men nev-er try._____

176

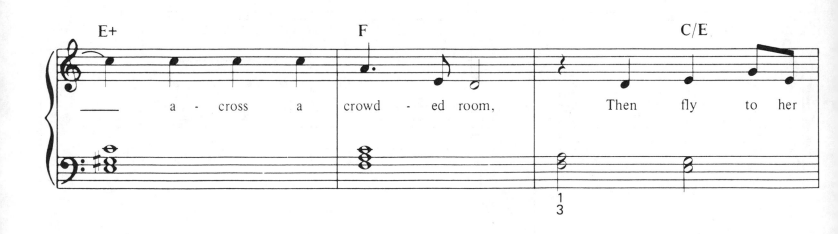

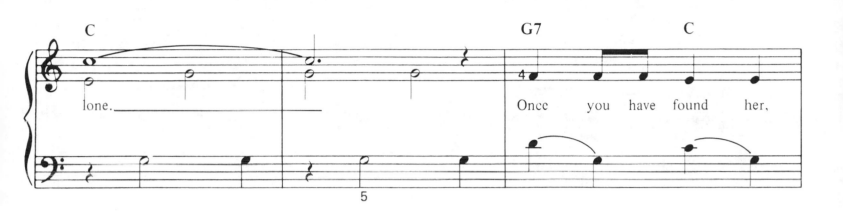

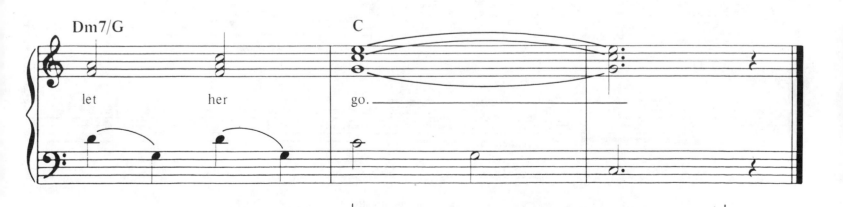

SOMETHING

Words and Music by
GEORGE HARRISON

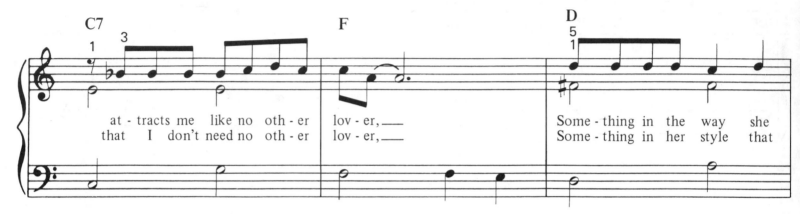

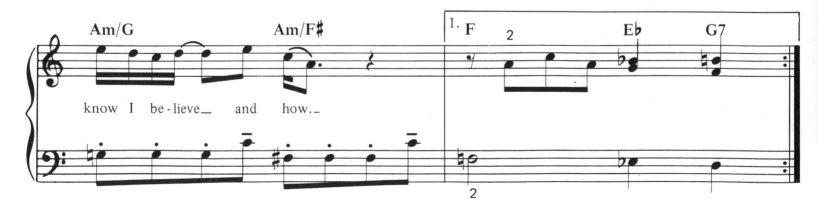

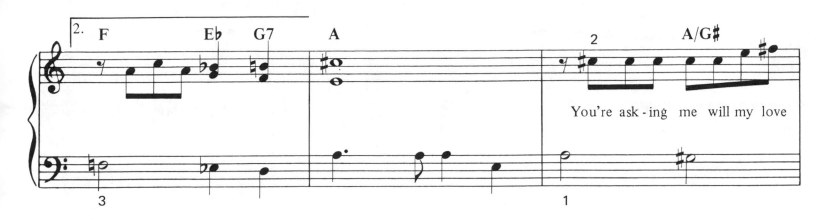

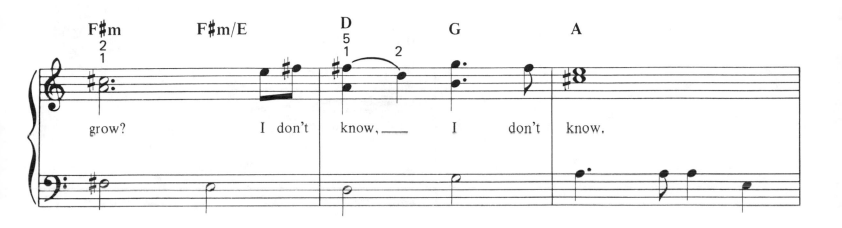

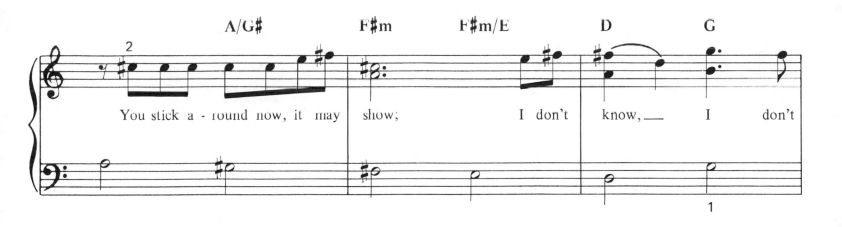

and all I have to do is think of her. Some-thing in the things she

shows __ me, I don't want to leave __ her now, you

know I be-lieve __ and how._

THROUGH THE YEARS

Words and Music by STEVE DORFF
and MARTY PANZER

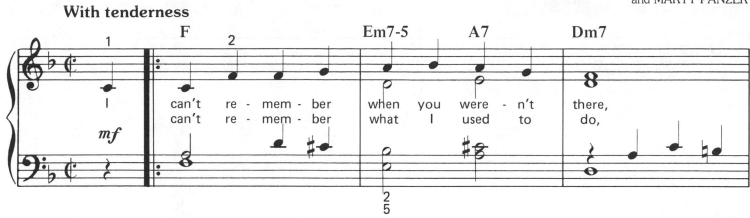

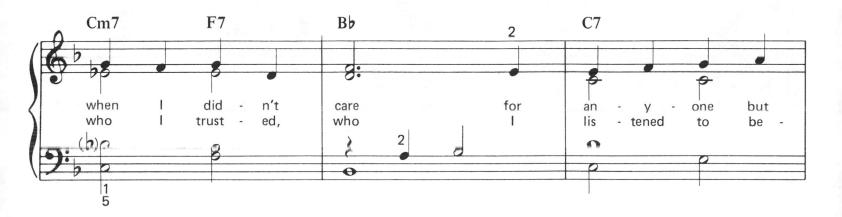

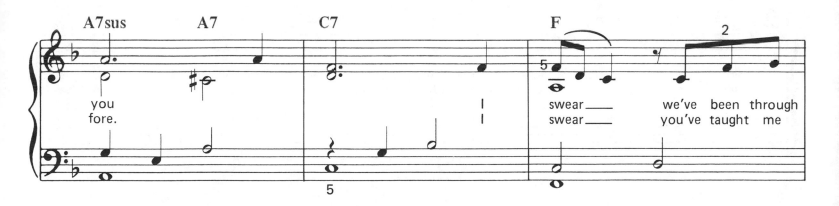

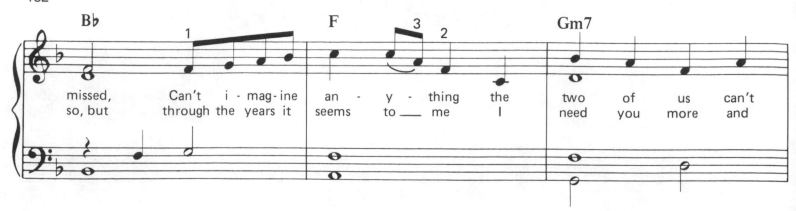

missed,   Can't i-mag-ine   an - y - thing   the   two   of   us   can't
so, but   through the years it   seems   to __ me   I   need   you   more   and

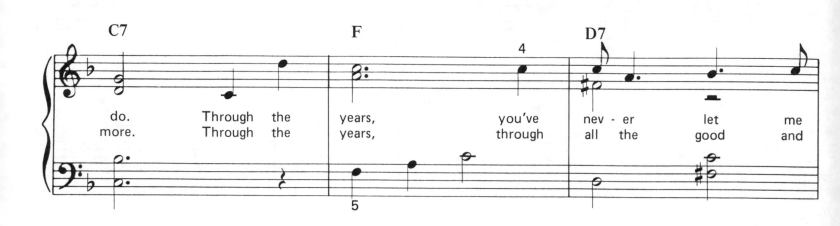

do.   Through   the   years,   you've   nev - er   let   me
more.   Through   the   years,   through   all   the   good   and

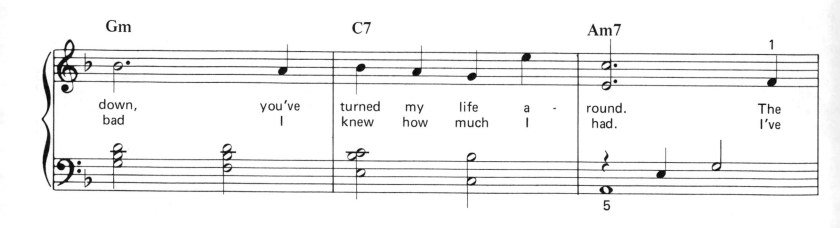

down,   you've   turned   my   life   a - round.   The
bad   I   knew   how   much   I   had.   I've

sweet - est   days   I've   found   I've found   with   you.   Through __ the
al - ways   been   so   glad   to   be   with   you.   Through __ the

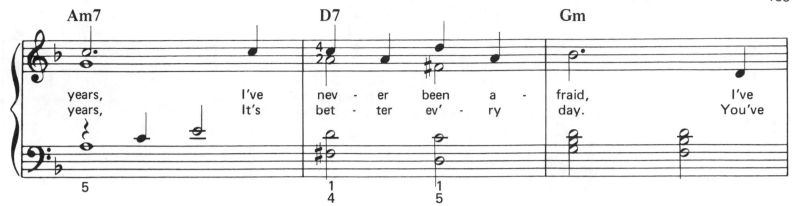

Am7   D7   Gm

years,   I've   nev - er   been   a -   fraid,   I've
years,   It's   bet - ter   ev' - ry   day.   You've

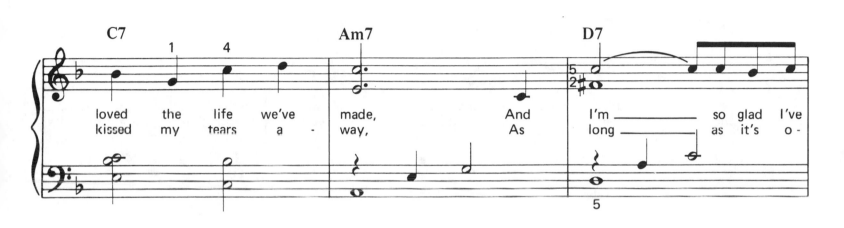

C7   Am7   D7

loved   the   life   we've   made,   And   I'm _____ so glad I've
kissed   my   tears   a -   way,   As   long _____ as it's o-

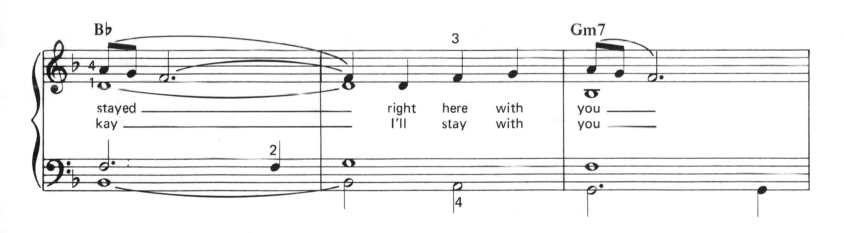

Bb   Gm7

stayed _____ right   here   with   you ____
kay _____ I'll   stay   with   you ____

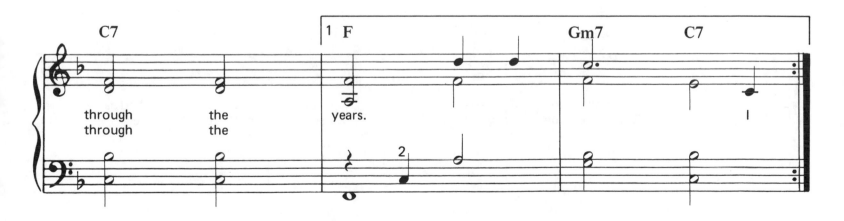

C7   1. F   Gm7   C7

through   the   years.
through   the

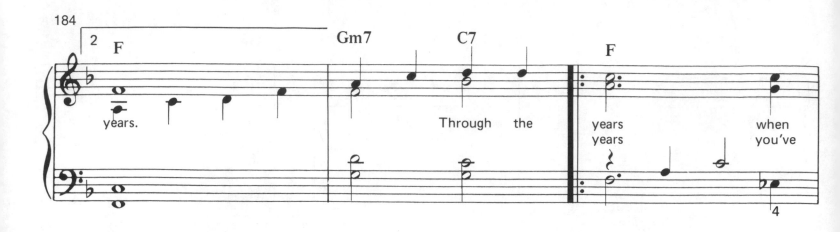

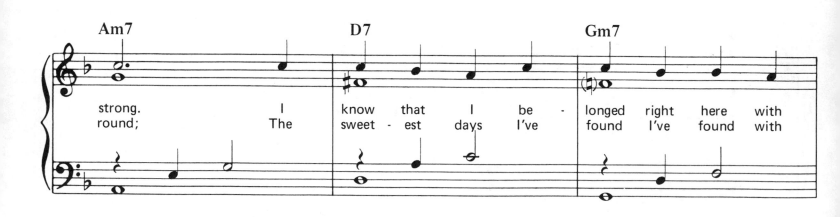

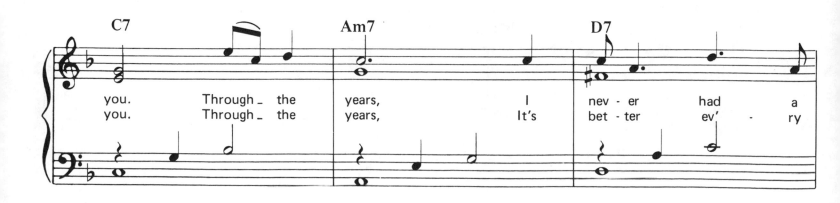

doubt we'd al - ways work things_ out I've
day, you've kissed my tears a - way As

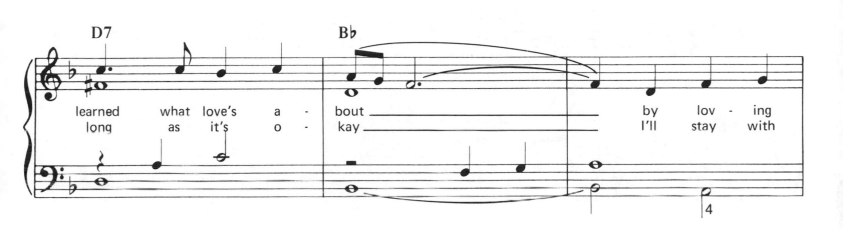

learned what love's a - bout_ by lov - ing
long as it's o - kay_ I'll stay with

you _ through the years.
you _ through the Through _ the

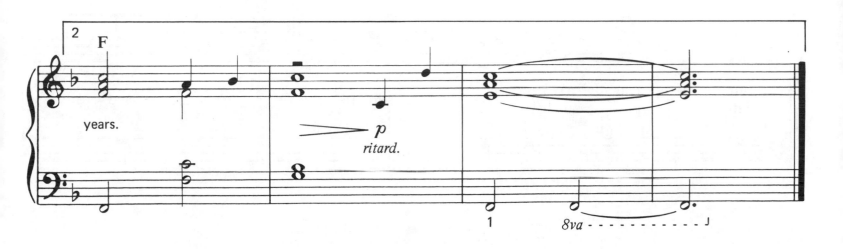

years.

ritard.

(You're My)
SOUL AND INSPIRATION

Words and Music by BARRY MANN
and CYNTHIA WEIL

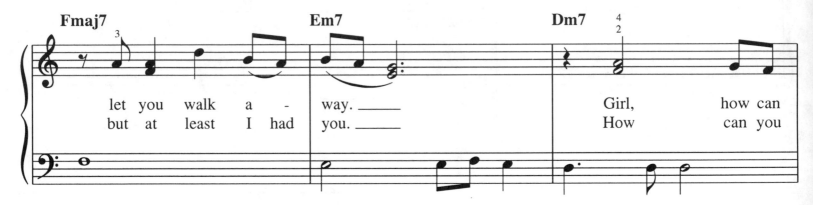

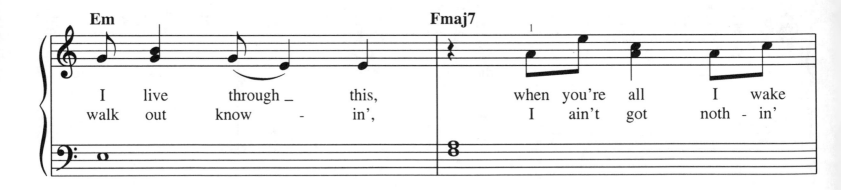

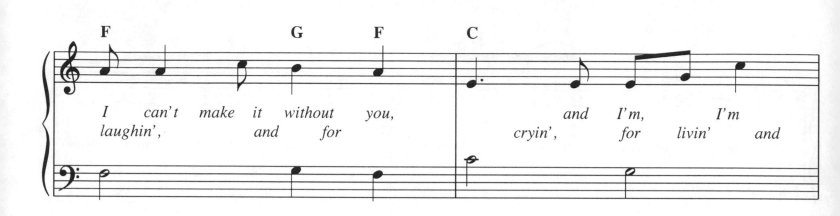

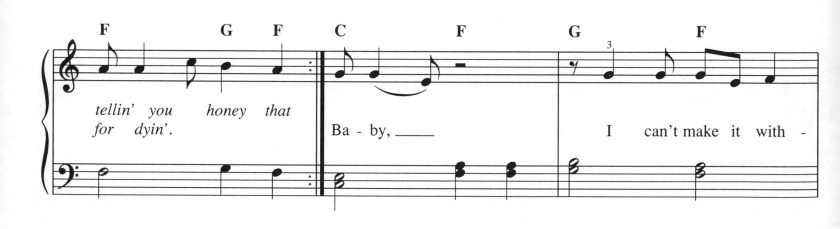

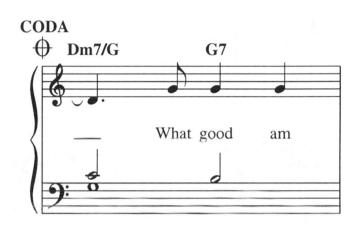

SUNRISE, SUNSET
from the Musical FIDDLER ON THE ROOF

Lyrics by SHELDON HARNICK
Music by JERRY BOCK

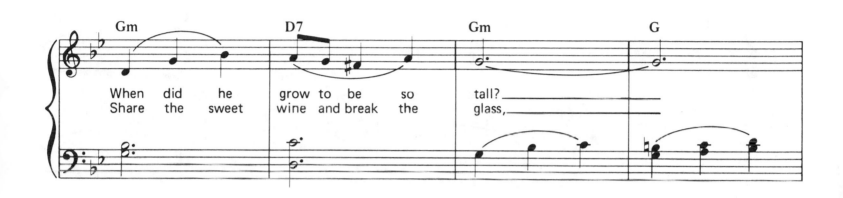
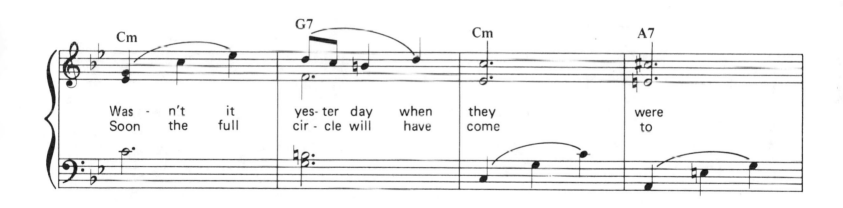

192

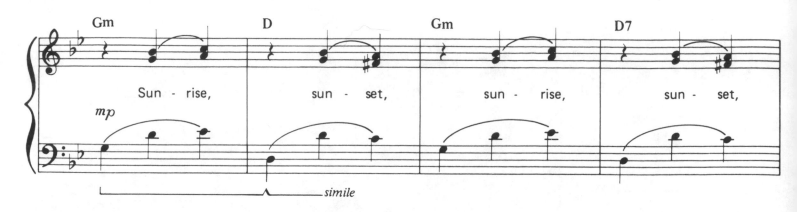

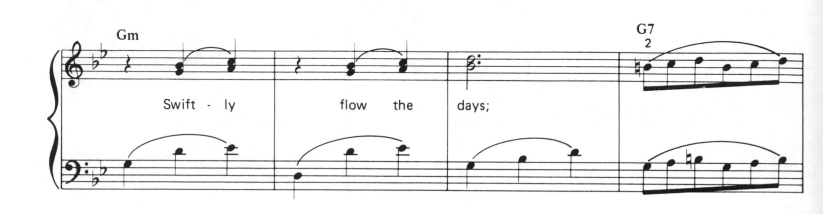

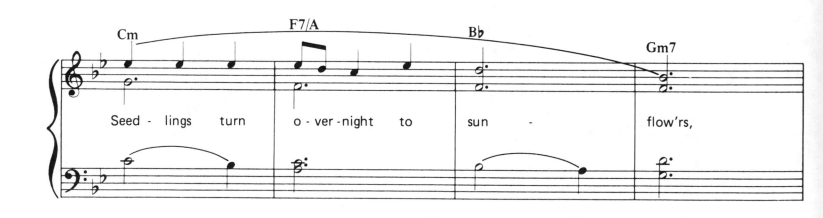

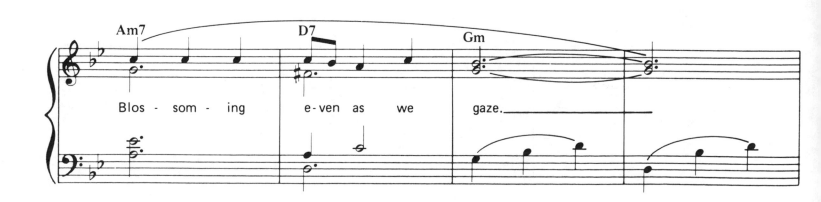

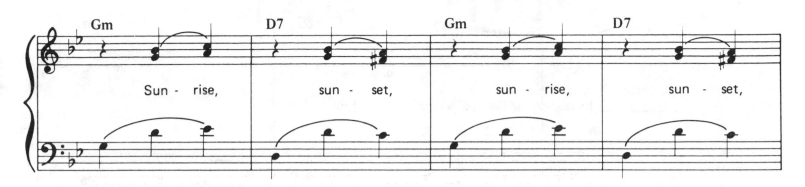

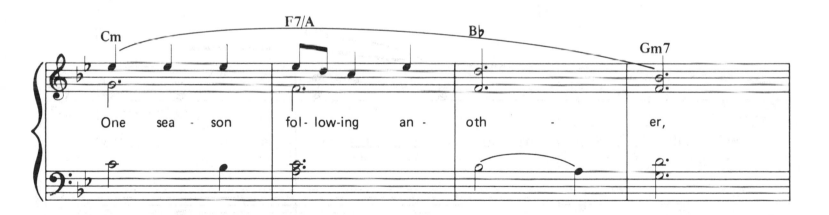

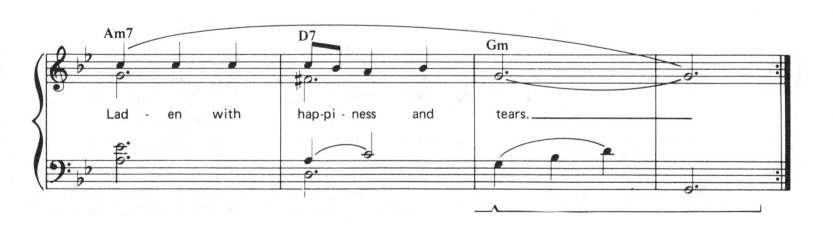

TO LOVE AGAIN
Theme from THE EDDY DUCHIN STORY

Based on Chopin's E Flat Nocturne
Words by NED WASHINGTON
Music by MORRIS STOLOFF and GEORGE SIDNEY

Moderate Waltz Tempo

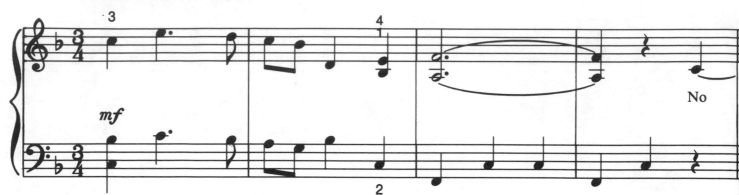

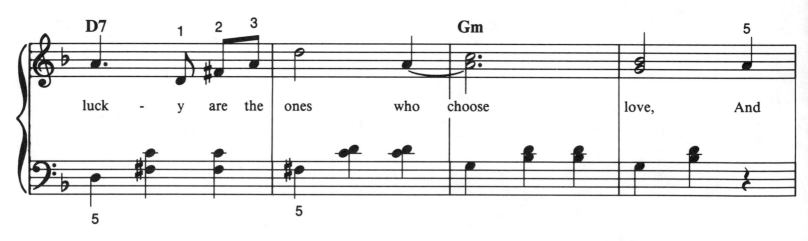

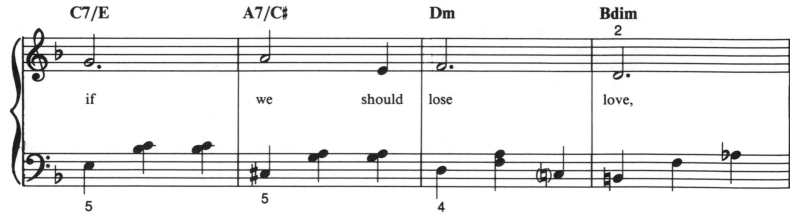

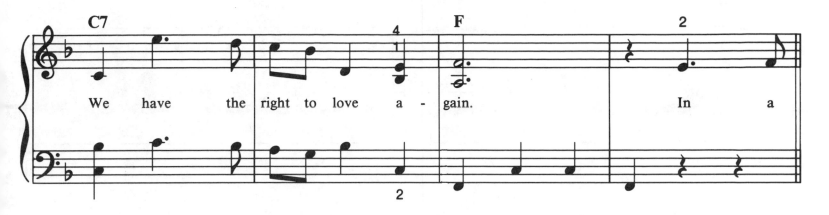

We have the right to love a - gain. In a

a little faster

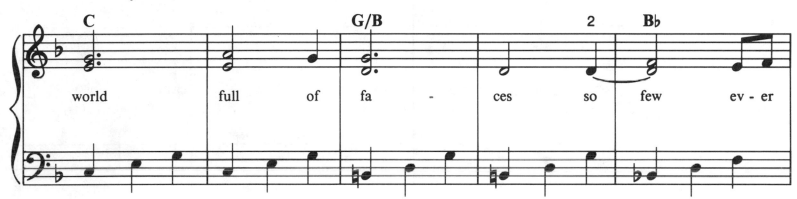

world full of fa - ces so few ev - er

find their pla - ces. In man - y

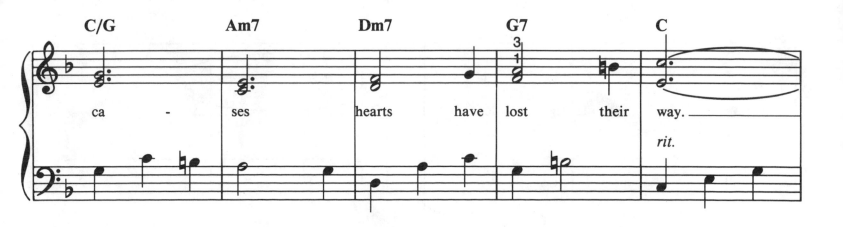

ca - ses hearts have lost their way.

rit.

Don't live_____ in the past,

a tempo

dear, For you and me the die is cast.

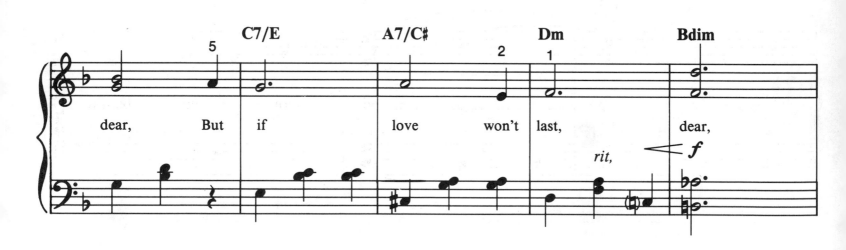

dear, But if love won't last, dear,

rit,

We have the right to love a - gain.

a tempo *rit.*

TRUE LOVE

Words and Music by
COLE PORTER

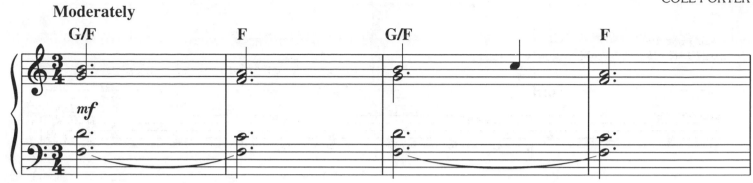

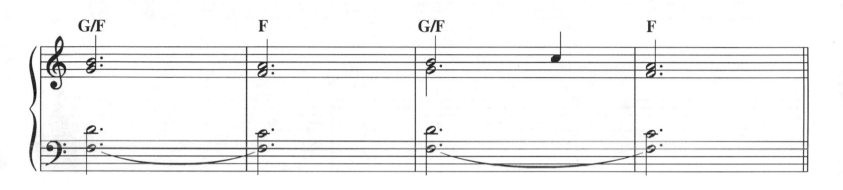

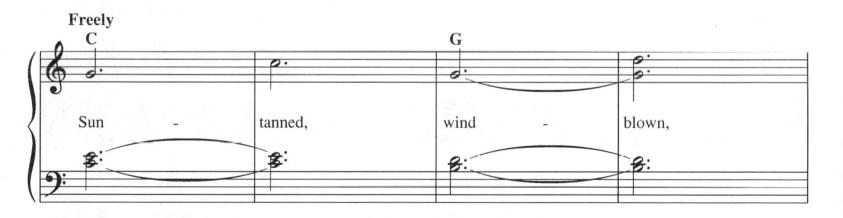

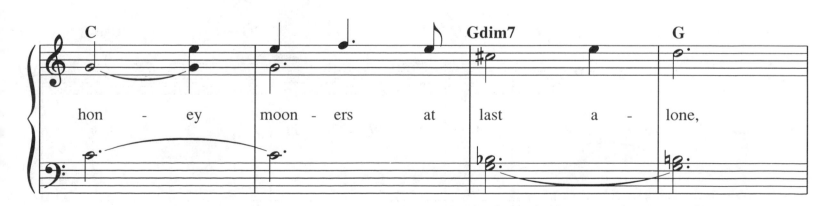

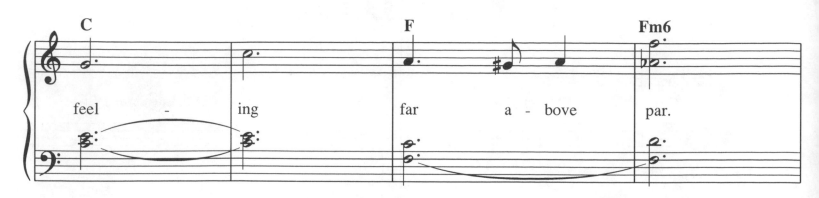

feel - ing far a - bove par.

Tempo 1

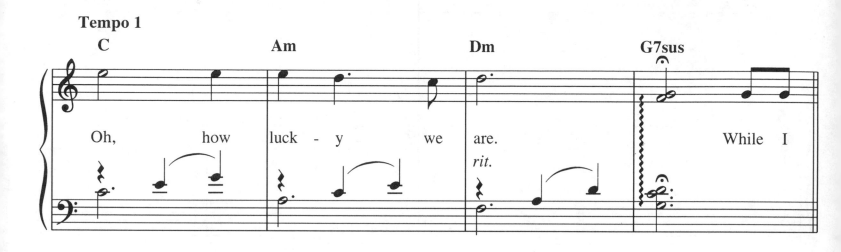

Oh, how luck - y we are. *rit.* While I

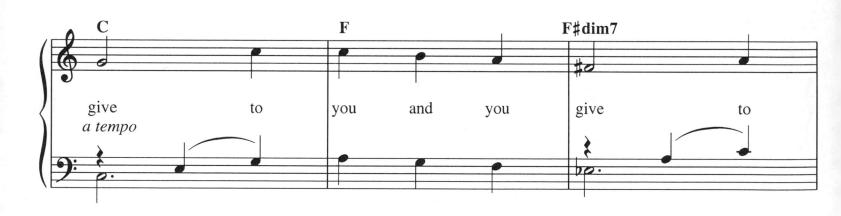

give to you and you give to
a tempo

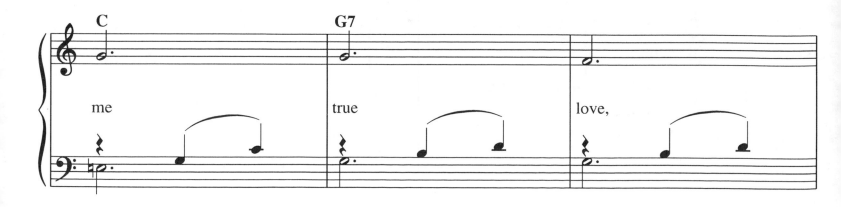

me true love,

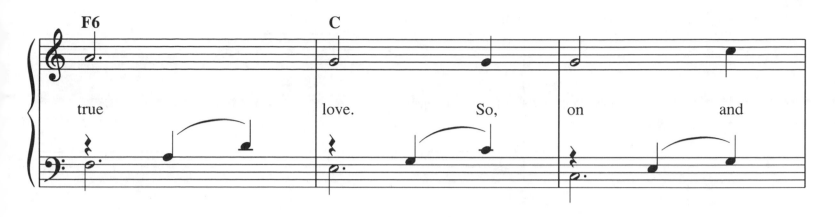

true ___ love. ___ So, on ___ and

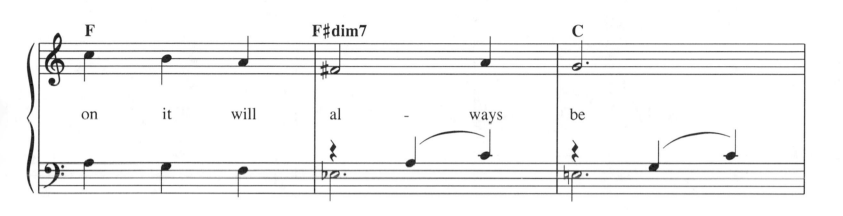

on it will al - ways be ___

true ___ love, ___ true

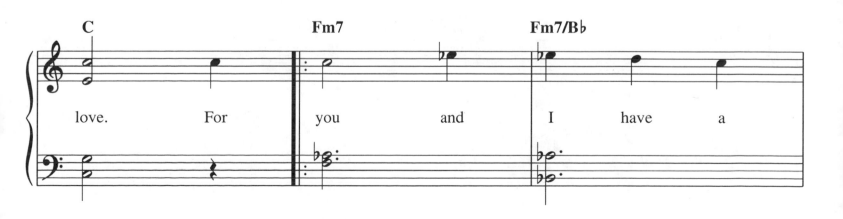

love. For you and I have a

guard - ian   an - gel   on   high   with

noth - ing   to   do.   But   to

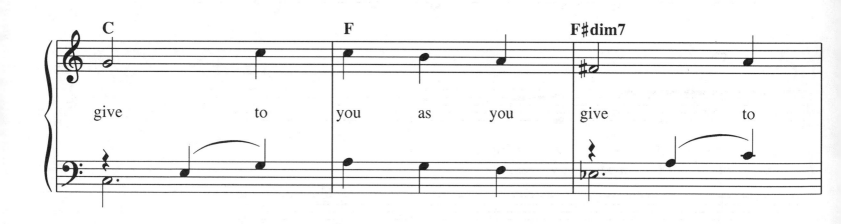

give   to   you   as   you   give   to

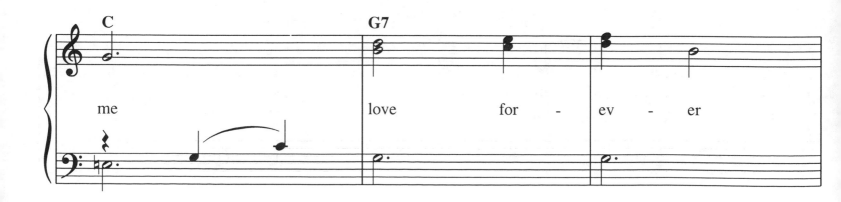

me   love   for - ev - er

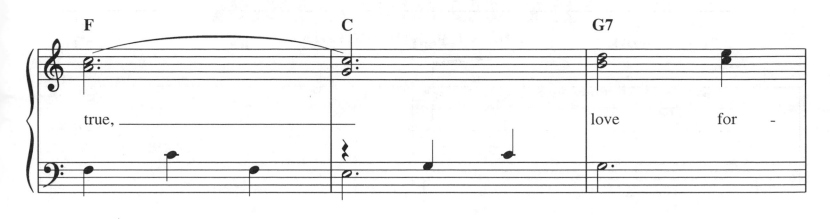

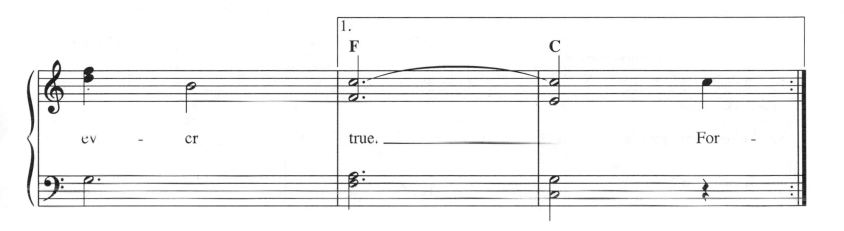

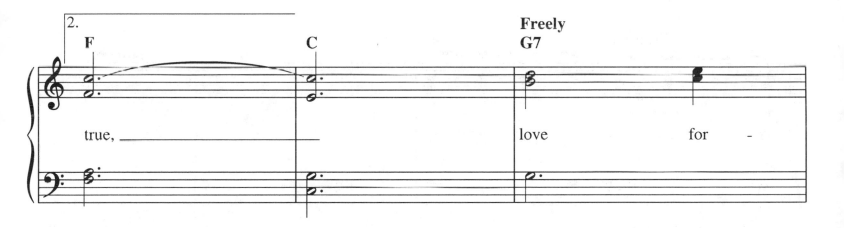

TRY TO REMEMBER
from THE FANTASTICKS

Words by TOM JONES
Music by HARVEY SCHMIDT

Slowly, with tenderness

Try to re - mem - ber the kind of Sep - tem - ber when
Try to re - mem - ber when life was so ten - der that

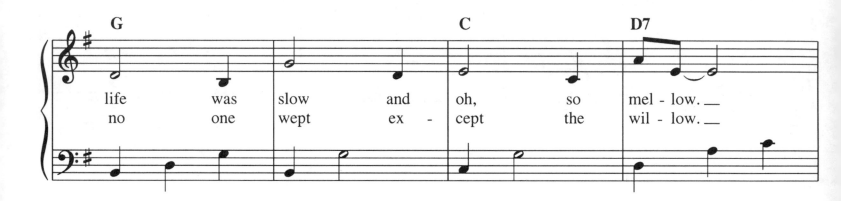

life was slow and oh, so mel - low. __
no one wept ex - cept the wil - low. __

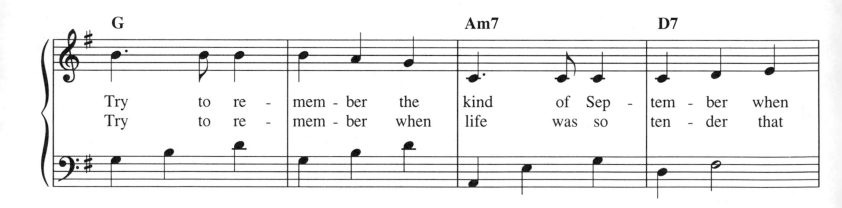

Try to re - mem - ber the kind of Sep - tem - ber when
Try to re - mem - ber when life was so ten - der that

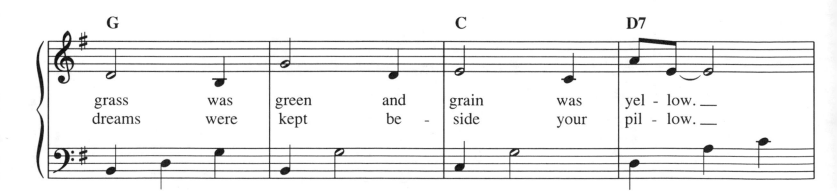

grass was green and grain was yel - low. __
dreams were kept be - side your pil - low. __

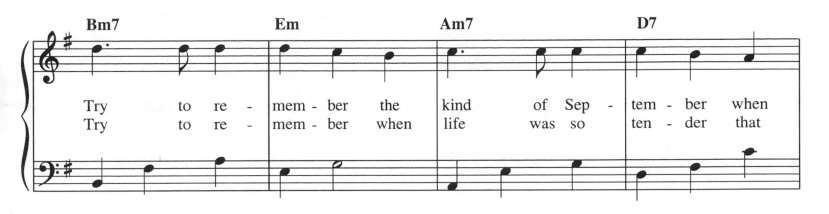

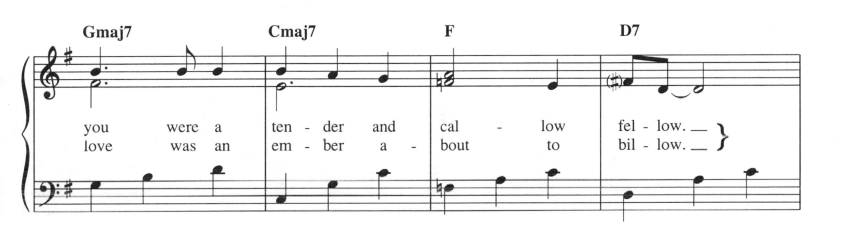

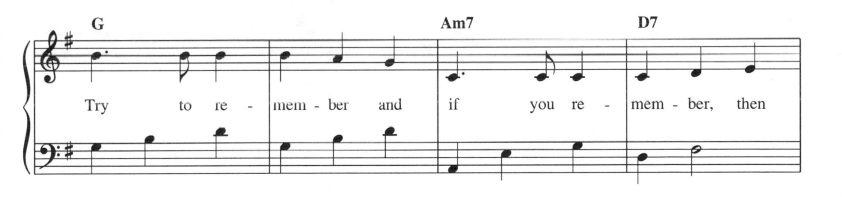

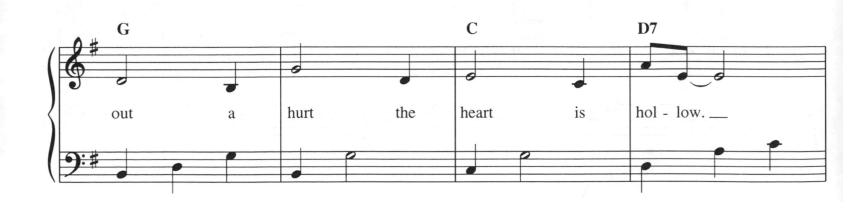

Deep in De - cem - ber, it's nice to re - mem - ber the fire of Sep -

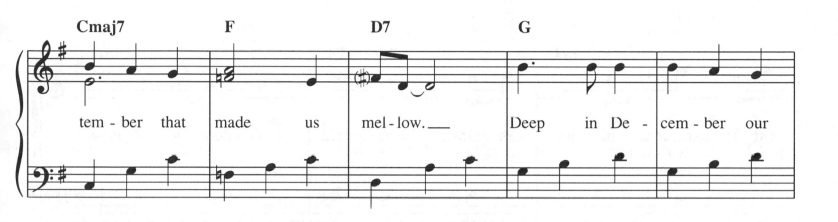

tem - ber that made us mel - low.___ Deep in De - cem - ber our

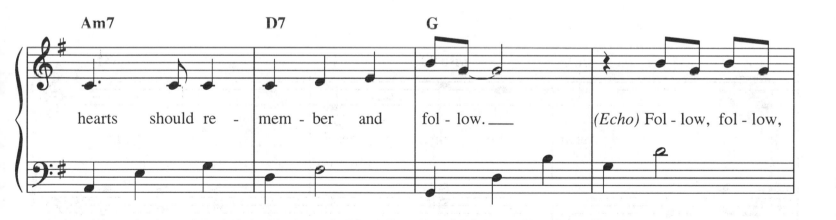

hearts should re - mem - ber and fol - low.___ *(Echo)* Fol - low, fol - low,

fol - low, fol - low, fol - low, fol - low, fol - low, fol - low, fol - low.___

VISION OF LOVE

Words and Music by MARIAH CAREY
and BEN MARGULIES

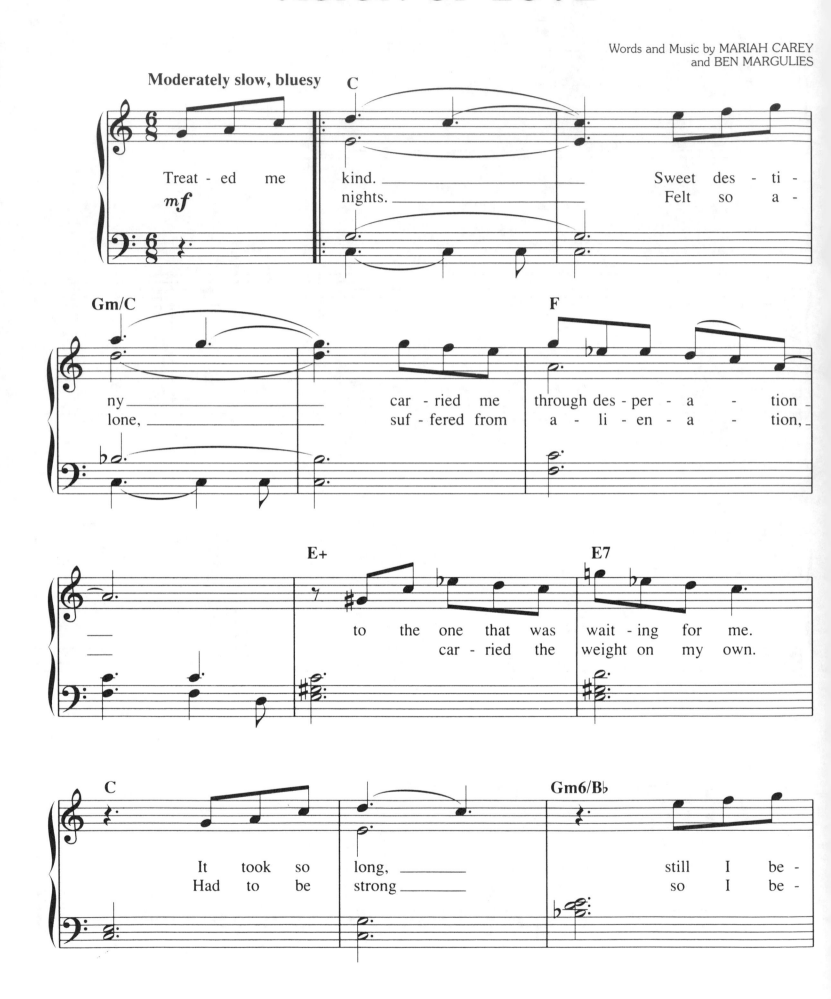

lieved _____
lieved _____

some - how the one that I need - ed
and now I know I've suc - ceed - ed

would ____ find me e - ven - tu - al - ly.
in _____ find - ing the place I con - ceived.

I had a vi - sion of love _____ and it was

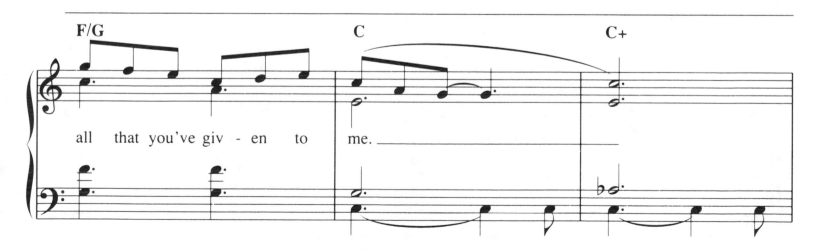

all that you've giv - en to me. _____

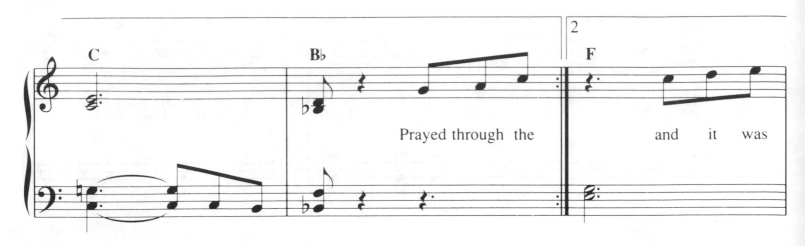

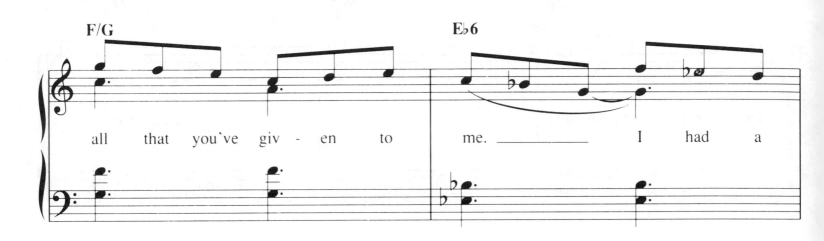

and I vi - su - al - ized _____ the

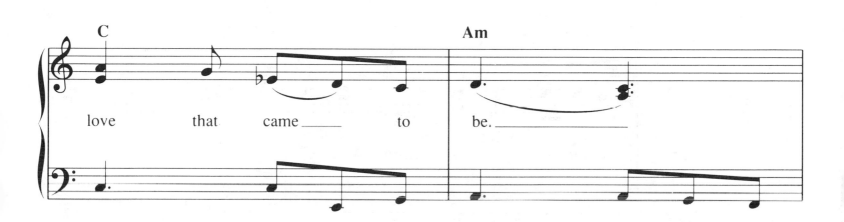

love that came ____ to be. _____

Feel _____ so a - live. _____ I'm so thank - ful that I've re -

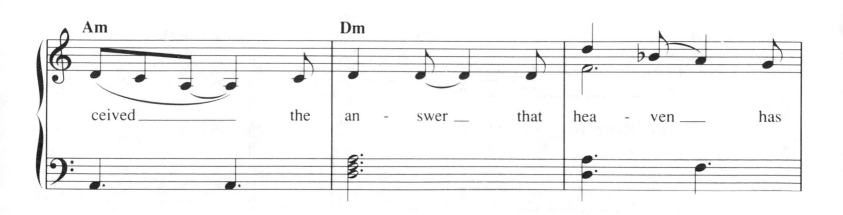

ceived _____ the an - swer __ that hea - ven ___ has

sent   down   to   me.   You treat - ed   me   kind, _____

_____ s - weet   des   -   ti - ny, _____

and   I'll   be   e - ter - nal - ly   grate - ful   hold - ing   you

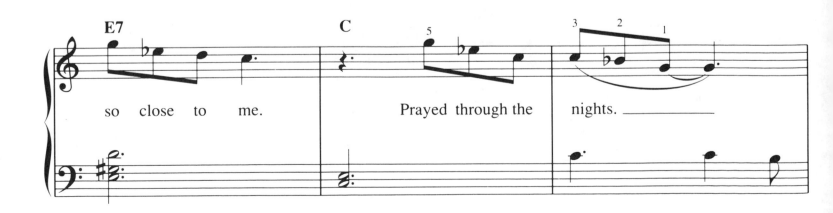

so   close   to   me.   Prayed through the   nights. _____

211

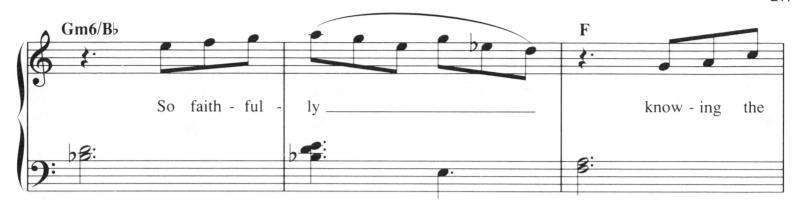

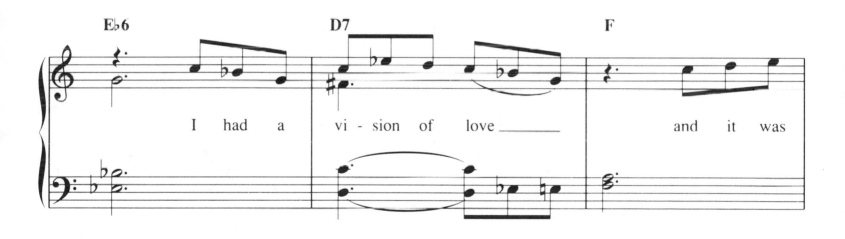

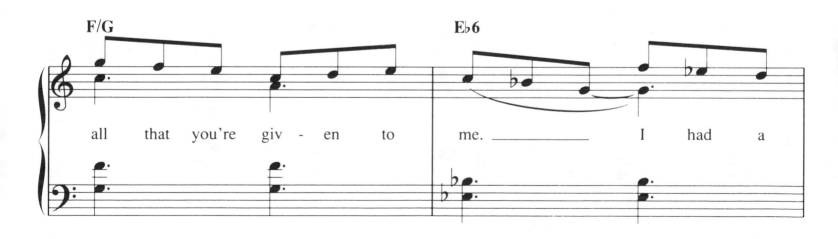

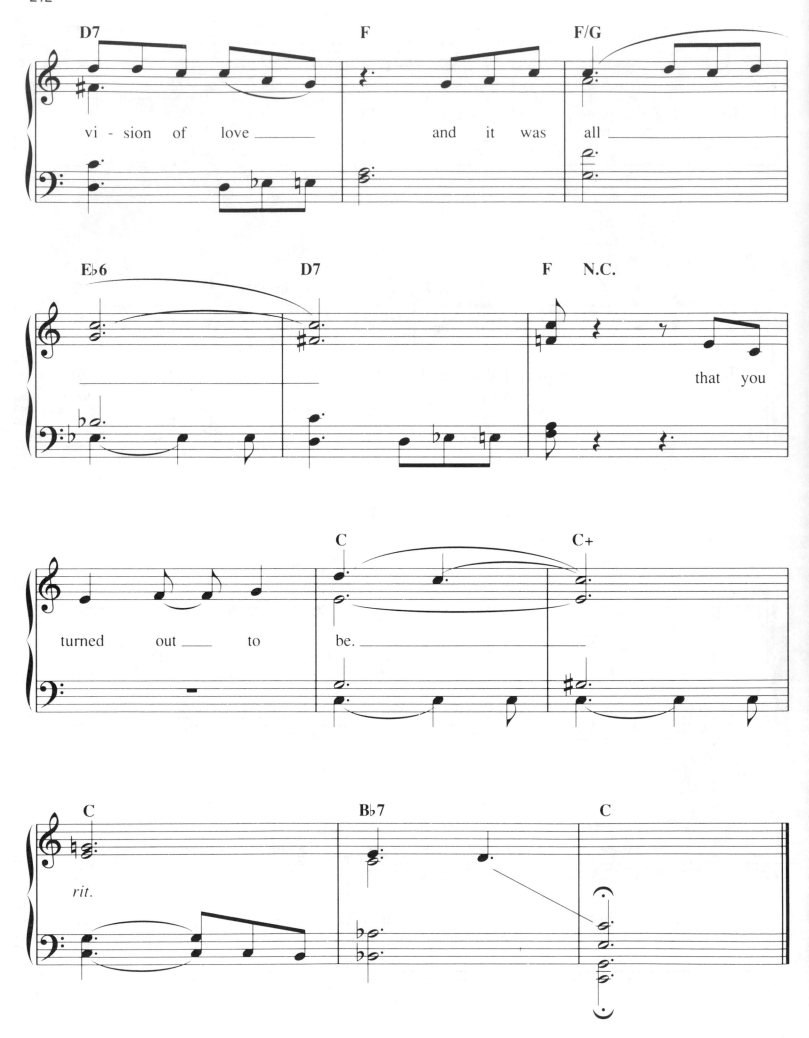

WHAT THE WORLD NEEDS NOW IS LOVE

Lyric by HAL DAVID
Music by BURT BACHARACH

214

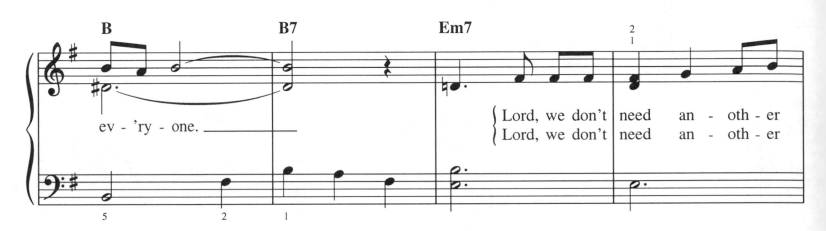

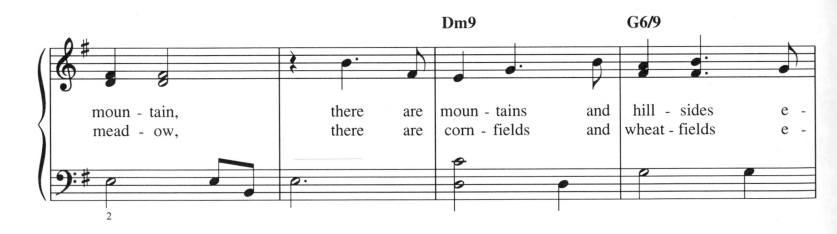

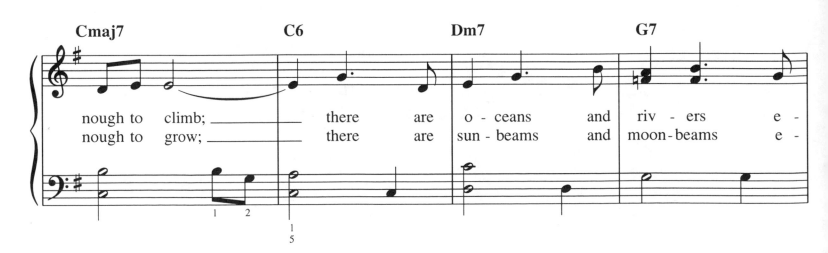

THE WAY WE WERE

from the Motion Picture THE WAY WE WERE

Words by ALAN and MARILYN BERGMAN
Music by MARVIN HAMLISCH

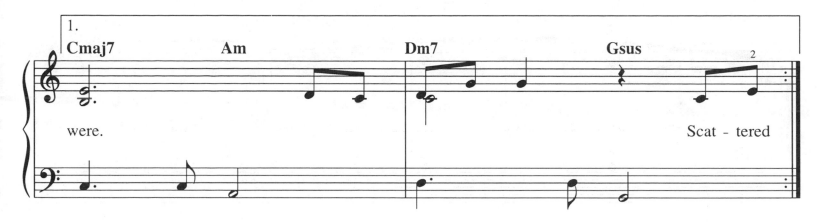

were.   Scat - tered

were.   Can it   be that it was all so

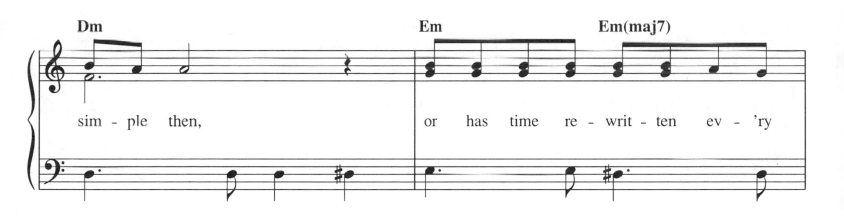

sim - ple then,   or   has time re - writ - ten ev - 'ry

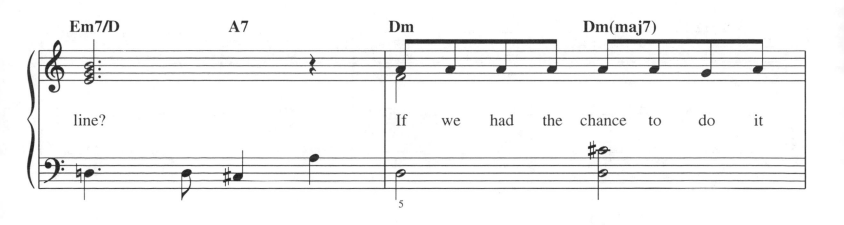

line?   If   we   had   the chance to   do   it

all a-gain, tell me would we? ___ Could we? ___

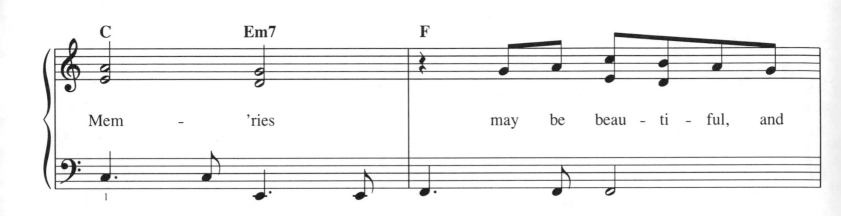

Mem - 'ries may be beau-ti-ful, and

yet, what's too pain-ful to re -

mem - ber we sim-ply choose to for - get.

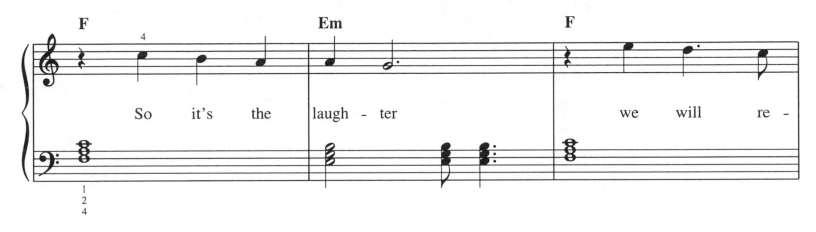

So it's the laugh - ter

we will re -

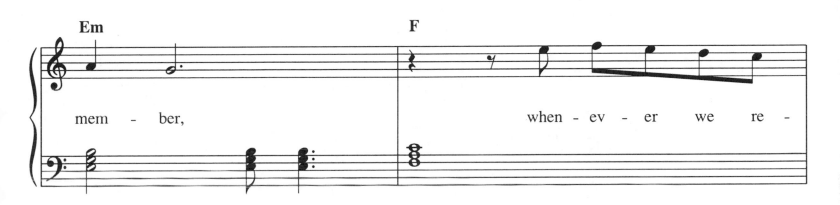

mem - ber,

when - ev - er we re -

mem - ber

the way we were;

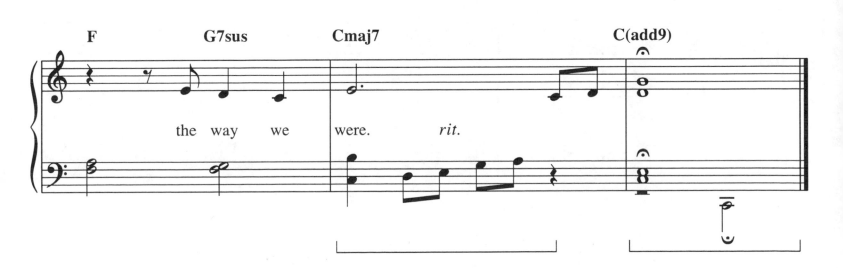

the way we were. *rit.*

WHEN I FALL IN LOVE

Words by EDWARD HEYMAN
Music by VICTOR YOUNG

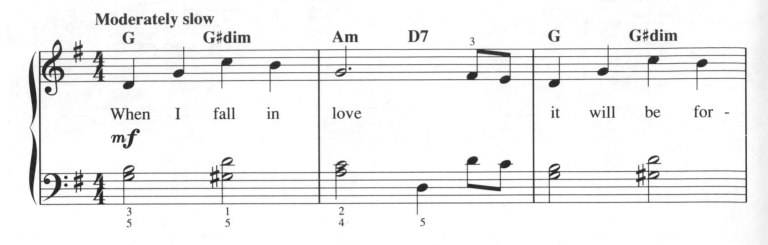

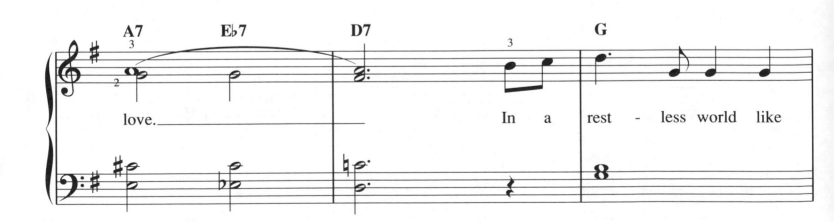

this is,   love is   end - ed be - fore it's be - gun,   and too

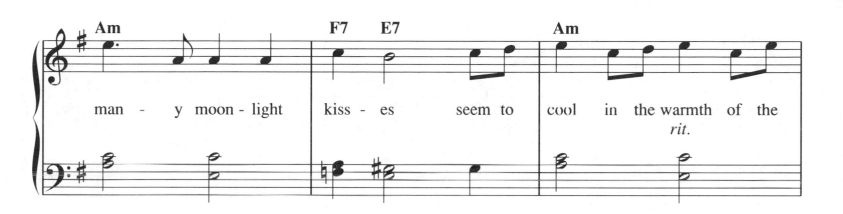

man - y moon - light   kiss - es   seem to   cool in the warmth of the
rit.

sun.   When I   give my   heart
a tempo

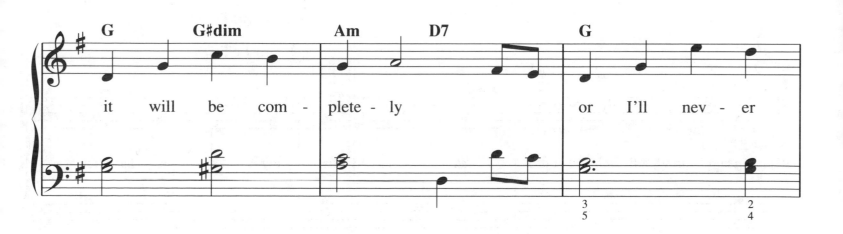

it will be com - plete - ly   or I'll nev - er

give my   heart.   And the

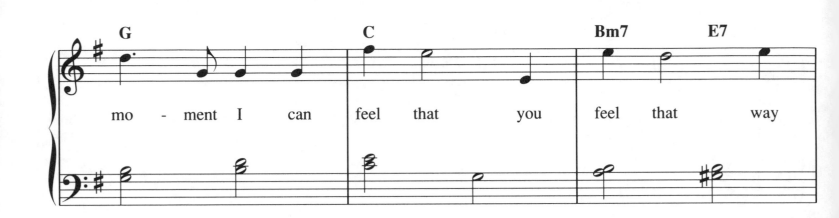

mo - ment I can   feel that   you   feel that   way

too   is   when I fall in   love   with

rit.   *a tempo*

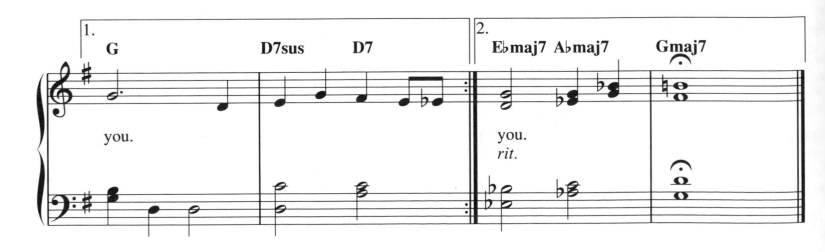

you.   you.

rit.

YOU GIVE GOOD LOVE

Words and Music by
LA FORREST "LA LA" COPE

MCA music publishing

know just what I need. It took some time for me to

see ___ that you give good love to me,

ba - by. So good. Take this heart of mine in - to your hands.

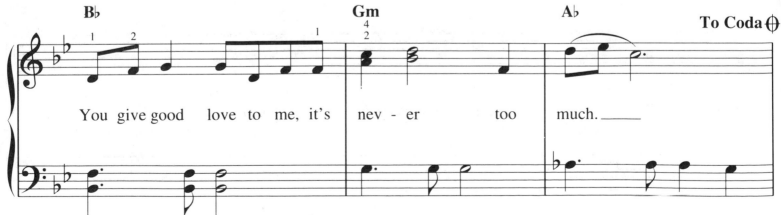

You give good love to me, it's nev - er too much. ___

WHEN I NEED YOU

Words by CAROLE BAYER SAGER
Music by ALBERT HAMMOND

Moderately, with feeling

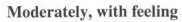

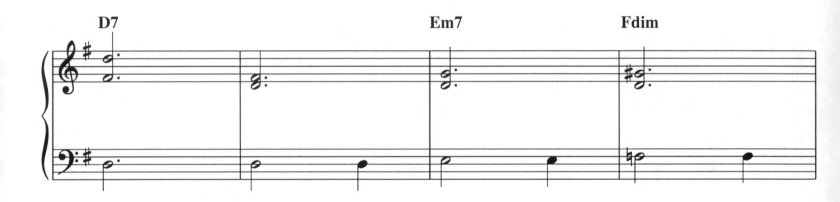

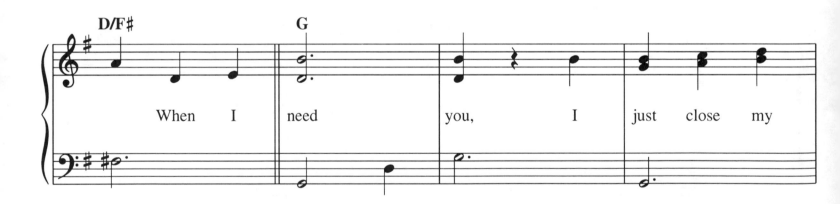

When I need you, I just close my

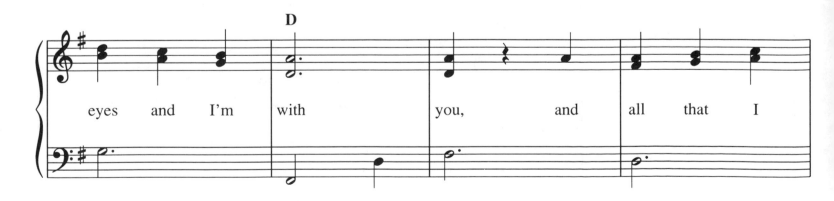

eyes and I'm with you, and all that I

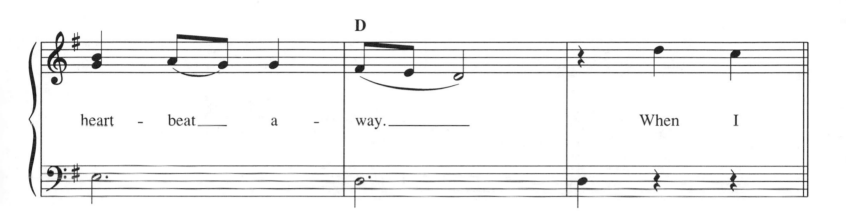

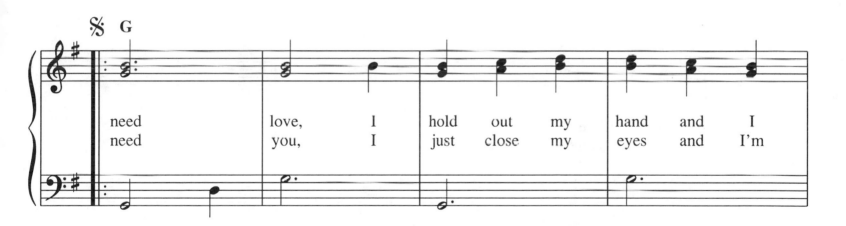

much give you, babe. love It's on - ly a keep - ing me warm night and heart - beat a -

day.
way.
Miles and miles of emp - ty
It's not eas - y when the

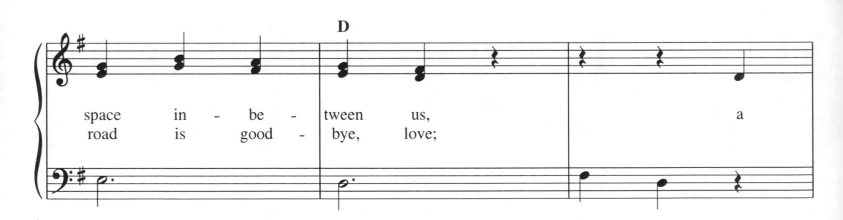

space in - be - tween us, a
road is good - bye, love;

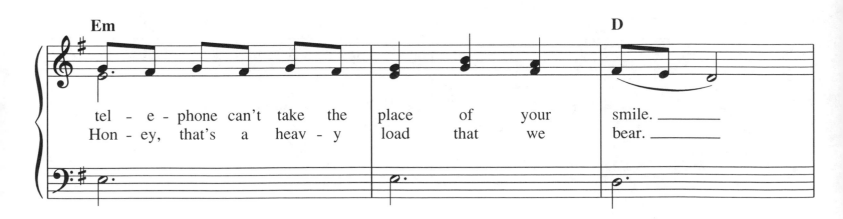

tel - e - phone can't take the place of your smile. _____
Hon - ey, that's a heav - y load that we bear. _____

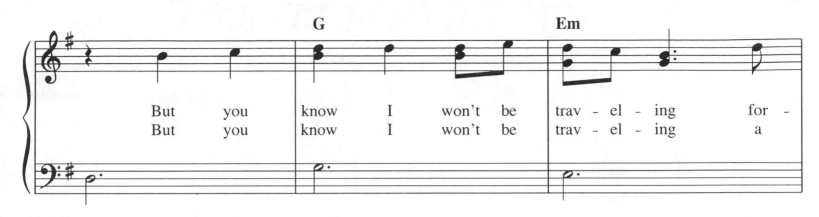

But you know I won't be trav - el - ing for -
But you know I won't be trav - el - ing a

ev - er. }
life - time. }

It's cold out, but

hold out and do like I do. When I

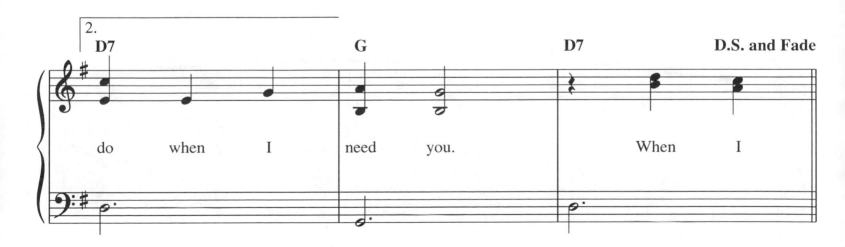

do when I need you. When I

WHERE DO I BEGIN
(Love Theme)
from the Paramount Picture LOVE STORY

Words by CARL SIGMAN
Music by FRANCIS LAI

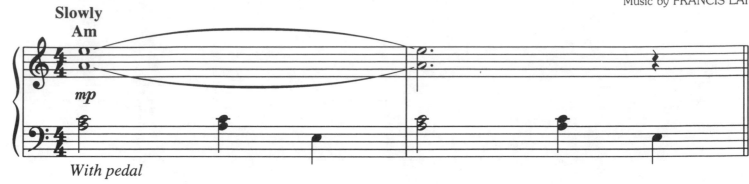

Slowly

With pedal

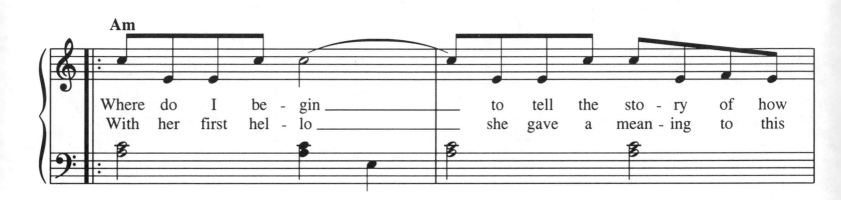

Where do I be - gin _____ to tell the sto - ry of how
With her first hel - lo _____ she gave a mean - ing to this

great a love can be, _____ the sweet love sto - ry that is
emp - ty world of mine; _____ there'd nev - er be an - oth - er

old - er than the sea, _____ the sim - ple truth a - bout the
love, an - oth - er time. _____ She came in - to my life and

love she brings to me? _____ Where do I start? _____
made the liv - ing fine. _____

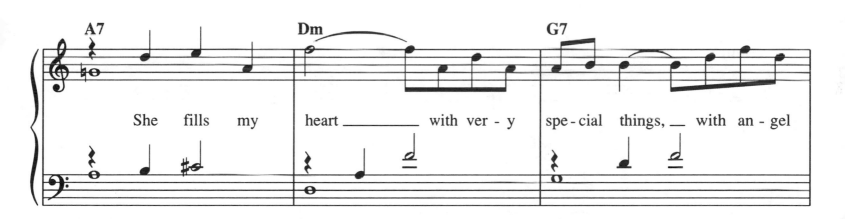

_____ _____ She fills my heart.

She fills my heart _____ with ver - y spe - cial things, __ with an - gel

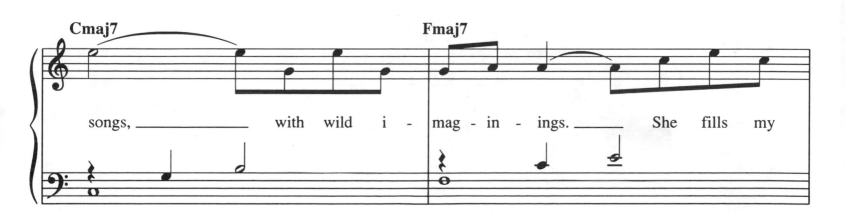

songs, _____ with wild i - mag - in - ings. _____ She fills my

soul _____ with so much love that an - y - where I

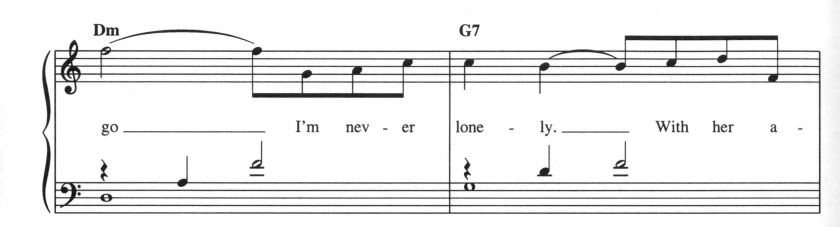

go _____ I'm nev - er lone - ly. _____ With her a -

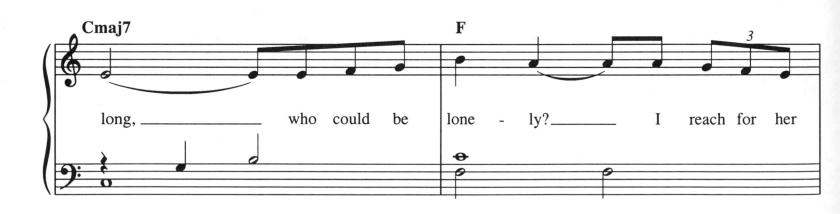

long, _____ who could be lone - ly? _____ I reach for her

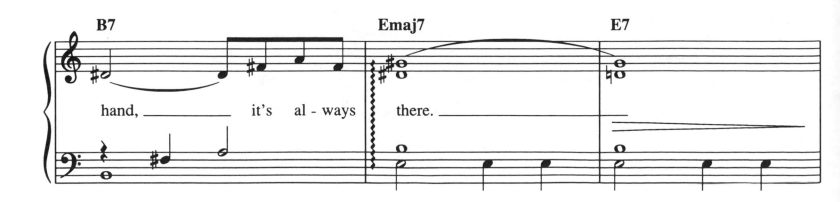

hand, _____ it's al - ways there. _____

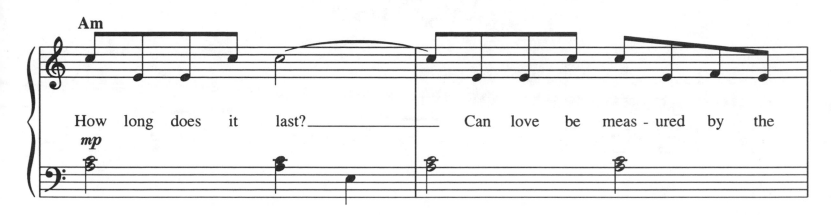

How long does it last?_____ Can love be meas-ured by the

hours __ in a day?_____ I have no an-swers now, but

this much I can say: _____ I know I'll need her 'til the stars all burn a-way,_____

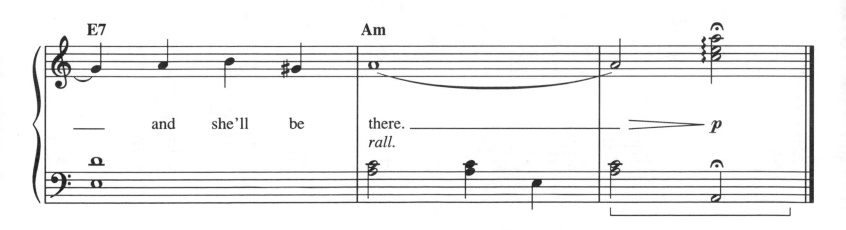

_____ and she'll be there._____ *p*
rall.

WOMAN

Words and Music by
JOHN LENNON

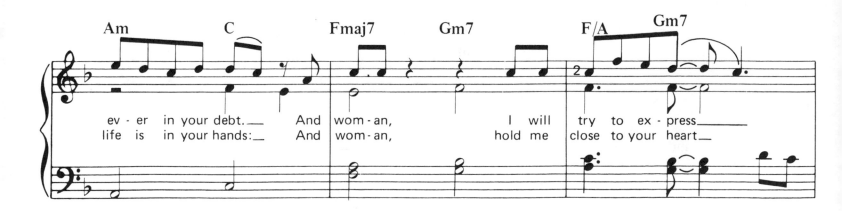

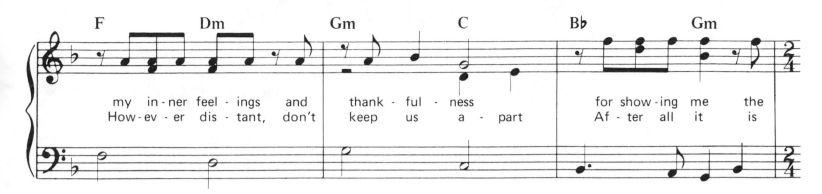

my in-ner feel-ings and thank-ful-ness for show-ing me the
How-ev-er dis-tant, don't keep us a - part Af - ter all it is

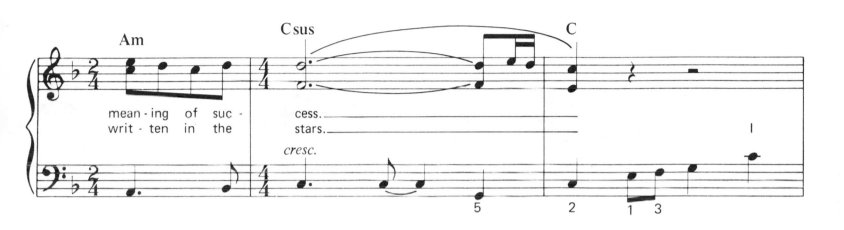

mean-ing of suc - cess.
writ-ten in the stars.

Ooh,_____ you, well, well. Doo doo doo
love_____ yeah, yeah, now and for -

doo doo.
ev - er.

rit. e dim.

YOU NEEDED ME

Words and Music by
RANDY GOODRUM

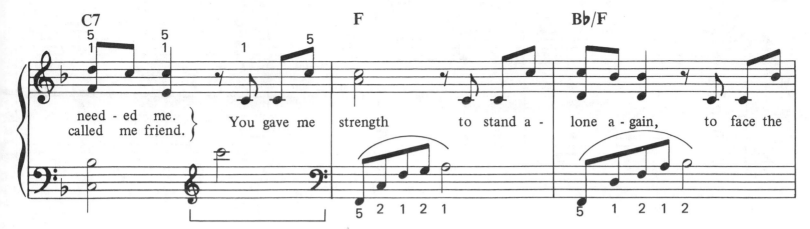

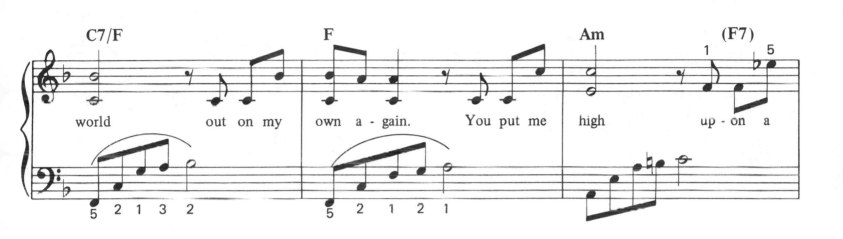

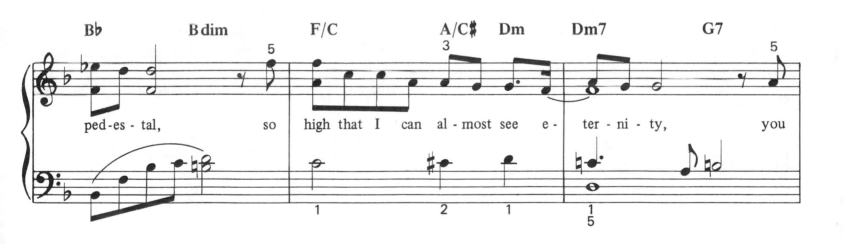

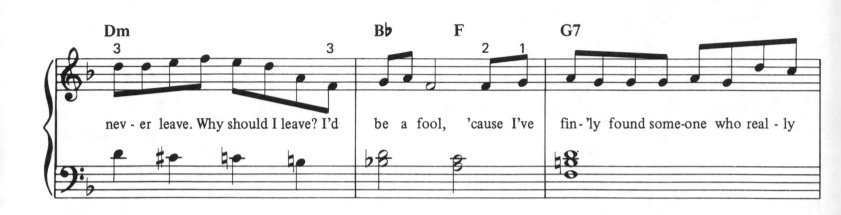

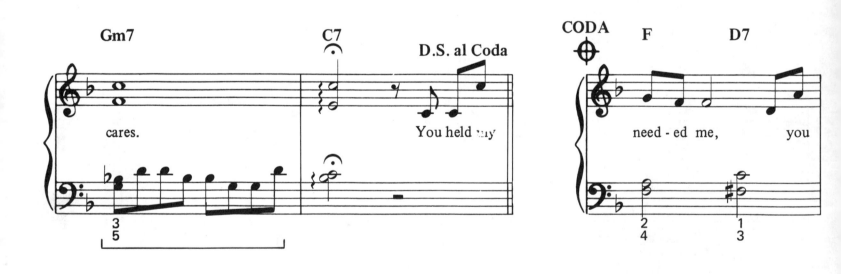

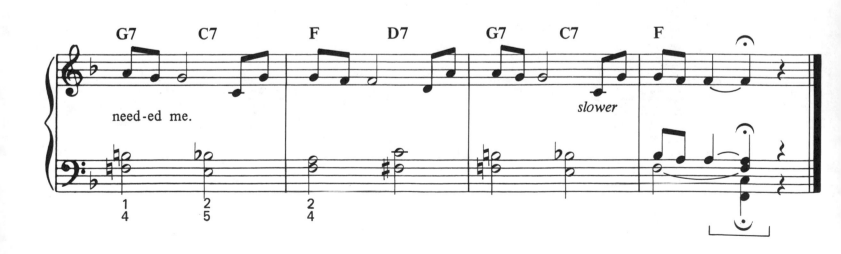

YOU'VE GOT A FRIEND

Words and Music by
CAROLE KING

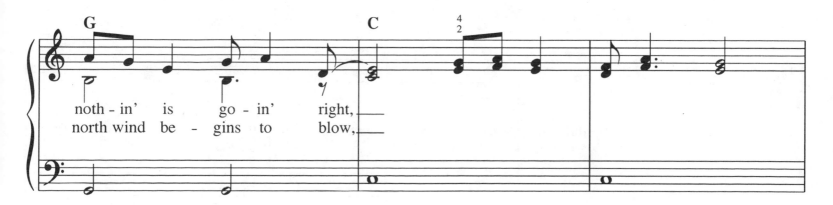

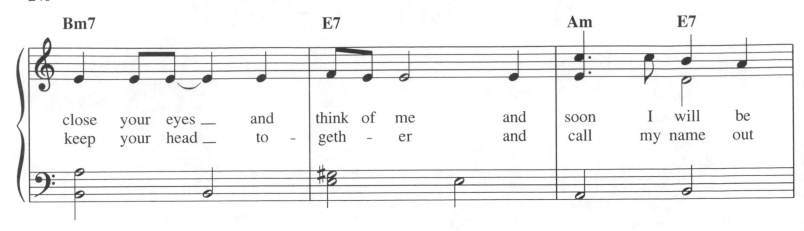

Bm7   E7   Am   E7

close your eyes __ and think of me and soon I will be
keep your head __ to - geth - er and soon call my name out

Am   E7   Am   Dm7   Em7

there to bright - en up ___ e - ven your dark - est nights.
loud; soon you'll hear ___ me knock - in' at your door. __

F/G   G   F/G   C

You just call out my ___ name __

F

___ and you know wher - ev - er I am I'll come run -

-nin' to see you a - gain.

Win - ter, spring, sum - mer and fall,

all you have to do is call and I'll

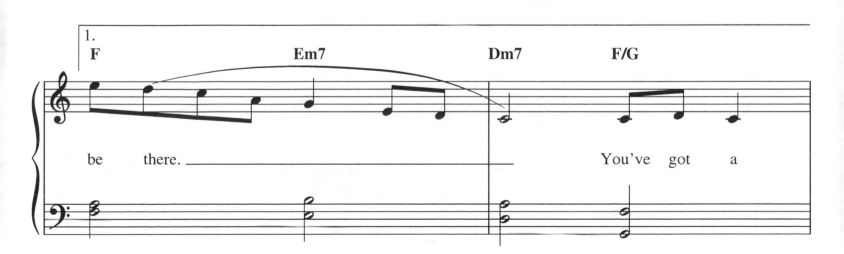

be there. You've got a

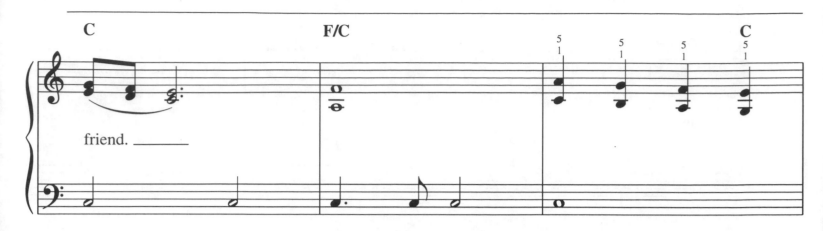

friend. _____

2.

If the be there, _____ yes, I will. ___ Now

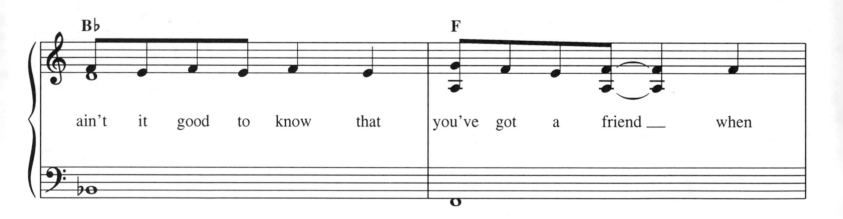

ain't it good to know that you've got a friend ___ when

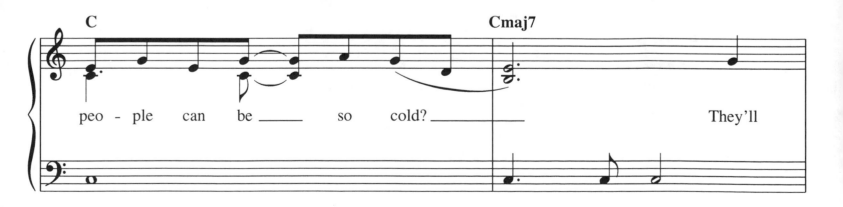

peo - ple can be ___ so cold? ___ They'll

hurt   you,   yes, and de - sert ____   you   and   take your   soul if you let

them.   Oh, but don't   you   let ____ them.   You just

CODA

be there _ yes I   will. ____   You've got   a   friend. ____

You've got   a   friend. ____   Ain't it   good to know you've got a

YOUR SONG

Words and Music by ELTON JOHN
and BERNIE TAUPIN

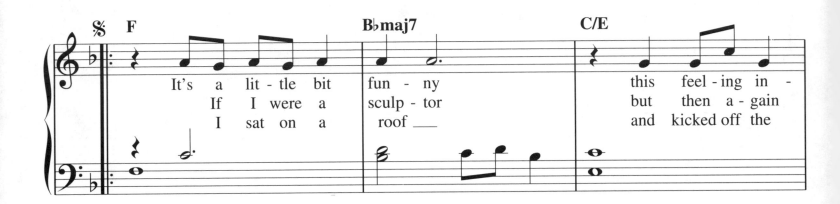

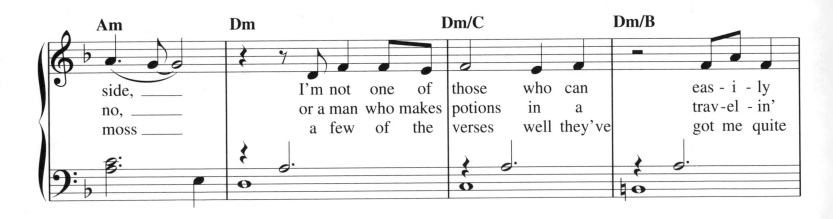

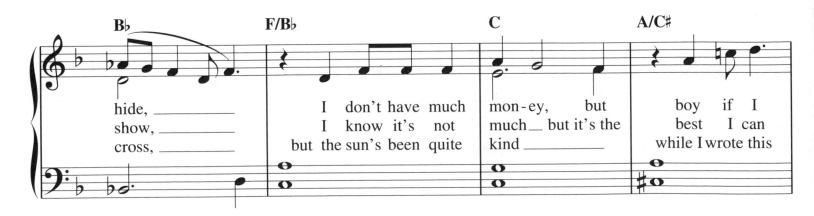

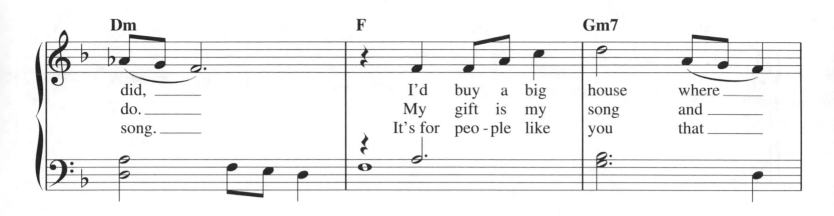

did, _____
do. _____
song. _____
I'd buy a big house where _____
My gift is my song and _____
It's for peo-ple like you that _____

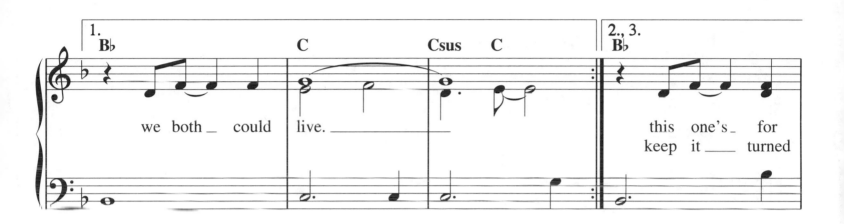

1.
we both _ could live. _____

2., 3.
this one's _ for
keep it _____ turned

you.
on.

cresc.

mf And you can tell

ev - 'ry-bod - y
this is your
song. _____

It may be quite____ sim - ple, but now that it's

done,____ I hope you don't mind, I hope you don't mind

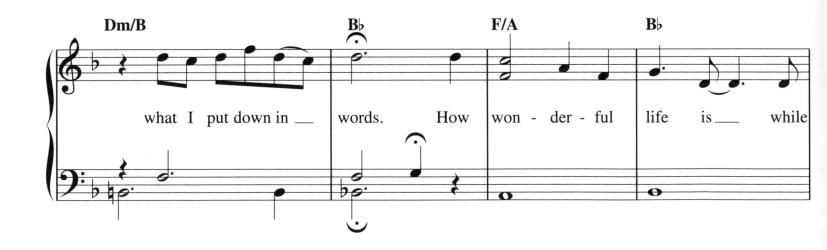

what I put down in __ words. How won - der - ful life is __ while

you're_ in the world._____

CODA

I hope you don't mind, I hope you don't mind

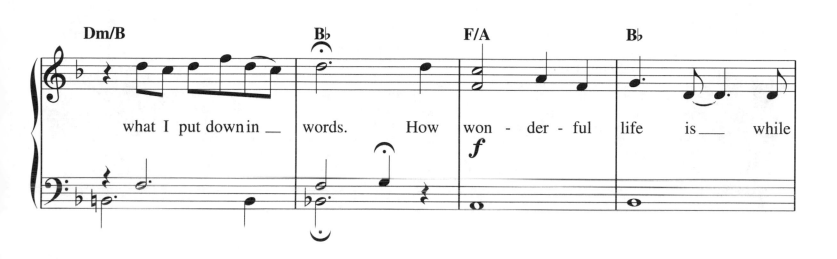

what I put down in ___ words. How won-der-ful life is ___ while

you're ___ in the world.

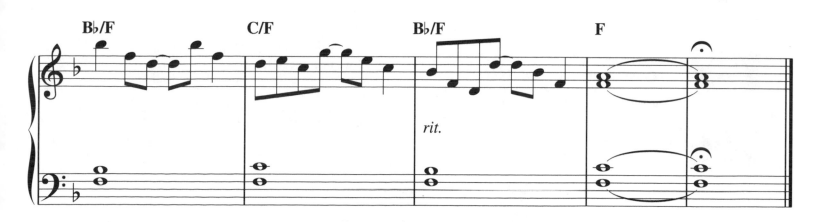

It's Easy To Play Your Favorite Songs
with Hal Leonard Easy Piano Books

Playing The Blues
Over 30 great blues tunes arranged for easy piano: Baby, Won't You Please Come Home • Chicago Blues • Fine And Mellow • Heartbreak Hotel • Pinetop's Blues • St. Louis Blues • The Thrill Is Gone • more.
00310102 ....$12.95

The Best Songs Ever
A prestigious collection of 80 all-time favorite songs, featuring: All I Ask Of You • Body And Soul • Candle In The Wind • Crazy • Don't Know Much • Endless Love • Feelings • Fly Me To The Moon • The Girl From Ipanema • Here's The Rainy Day • Imagine • In The Mood • Let It Be • Longer • Moonlight In Vermont • People • Satin Doll • Save The Best For Last • Some Enchanted Evening • Somewhere Out There • Stormy Weather • Strangers In The Night • Tears In Heaven • What A Wonderful World.
00359223 ....$18.95

Country Love Songs
34 classic and contemporary country favorites, including: The Dance • A Few Good Things Remain • Forever And Ever Amen • I Never Knew Love • Love Can Build A Bridge • Love Without End, Amen • She Believes In Me • She Is His Only Need • Where've You Been • and more.
00110030 ....$12.95

Movie Favorites For Easy Piano
Over 15 familiar theme songs, such as: Beauty And The Beast • Candle On The Water • Endless Love • Kokomo • The Rainbow Connection • Somewhere Out There • Unchained Melody • Under The Sea • and more.
00222551 ....$8.95

Miss Saigon
11 songs from this Broadway epic, including: The American Dream • The Heat Is On In Saigon • I'd Give My Life For You • The Last Night Of The World • Sun And Moon • and more.
00222537 ....$14.95

Rock N Roll For Easy Piano
40 rock favorites for the piano, including: All Shook Up • At The Hop • Chantilly Lace • Great Balls Of Fire • Lady Madonna • The Shoop Shoop Song (It's In His Kiss) • The Twist • Wooly Bully • and more.
00222544..$12.95

I'll Be Seeing You
50 Songs Of World War II
A salute to the music and memories of WWII, including a chronology of events on the homefront, dozens of photos, and 50 radio favorites of the GIs and their families back home. Includes: Boogie Woogie Bugle Boy • Don't Sit Under The Apple Tree (With Anyone Else But Me) • I Don't Want To Walk Without You • Moonlight In Vermont • and more.
00310147..$17.95

Disney's The Hunchback Of Notre Dame Selections
10 selections from Disney's animated classic, complete with beautiful color illustrations. Includes: The Bells Of Notre Dame • God Help The Outcasts • Out There • Someday • and more.
00316011...$14.95

Today's Love Songs
31 contemporary favorites, including: All I Ask Of You • Because I Love You • Don't Know Much • Endless Love • Forever And Ever, Amen • Here And Now • I'll Be Loving You Forever • Lost In Your Eyes • Love Without End, Amen • Rhythm Of My Heart • Unchained Melody • Vision Of Love • and more.
00222541...$14.95

Best Of Cole Porter
Over 30 songs, including: Be A Clown • Begin The Beguine • Easy To Love • From This Moment On • In The Still Of The Night • Night And Day • So In Love • Too Darn Hot • You Do Something To Me • You'd Be So Nice To Come Home To • and more
00311576...$14.95

FOR MORE INFORMATION, SEE YOUR LOCAL MUSIC DEALER,
OR WRITE TO:

HAL•LEONARD®
CORPORATION
7777 W. BLUEMOUND RD. P.O. BOX 13819 MILWAUKEE, WI 53213

Prices, book contents, and availability subject to change without notice

0796